IN THE

NEW AFRICAN CANADIAN LITERATURE

BLACK

IN THE

NEW AFRICAN CANADIAN LITERATURE

BLACK

edited by

ALTHEA PRINCE

INSOMNIAC PRESS

Library and Archives Canada Cataloguing in Publication
In the black : new African Canadian literature / [edited by]
Althea Prince.

ISBN 978-1-55483-085-5

1. Canadian literature (English)--Black-Canadian authors.
2. Canadian literature (English)--21st century. I. Prince, Althea, 1945-

PS8235.B53I5 2012   C810.8'0896071   C2012-905392-9

The publisher gratefully acknowledges the support of
the Canada Council, the Ontario Arts Council,
and the Department of Canadian Heritage through the
Canada Book Fund.

Printed and bound in Canada

Insomniac Press
520 Princess Avenue, London, Ontario, Canada, N6B 2B8
www.insomniacpress.com

I dedicate this collection to two African Canadian writers in whose shoes it walks. I am referring to poet and novelist, Dr. George Elliott Clarke, and playwright, Djanet Sears. Both Clarke and Sears have published healthy collections of African Canadians' writing, and have also produced their own contributions to the cultural lexicon of Canada. I am delighted to include both authors in this collection.

—Dr. Althea Prince

I am thankful to all of the contributors for taking the time to create and submit their work. Without exception, the authors in this collection have been generous with their time, and consistent in their attention to the details demanded of them to move the collection to publication. I appreciate their creative work, and the peace and ease of their temperaments.

I gratefully acknowledge the usual deft editing of the folks at Insomniac Press. Editor Gillian Buckley exercised diligence and care in going over the manuscript. I am also grateful to Gillian Rodgerson for her dexterous proofreading. And as usual, my thanks to Publisher, Mike O'Connor for believing in the project.

—Dr. Althea Prince

CONTENTS

INTRODUCTION

Dr. Althea Prince

This collection consists of fresh writing from a number of authors. The book is consciously intergenerational, and is a "mix" of genres. The objective is to bring together writers of short fiction, poetry, dub poetry, and hip hop.

The focus in the collection is on the authors' subjectivities—all will contribute to an expanded vision of African Canadian literature. The cultural and historical landscape is a vibrant part of the African Canadian imaginary, and is reflected in the writing of the authors whose work is included in the anthology. The collection contains the work of two Governor General's Award winners, a winner of two Gemini Awards, and other award-winning writers.

The fiction writers are interesting in the range of their focus, and also their background. Djanet Sears, a Governor General's Award winner, has made her name in the cultural landscape as a playwright, and as an actor, both in film and onstage. She has included fiction and poetry in the collection, another rarity that is important to make noteworthy. Joanne Hillhouse is well-known in Toronto circles, having graced Toronto stages to read from her work on several occasions. She resides in Antigua, and has recently published her third novel, *Oh Gad!*

Catherine Bain and Gayle Gonsalves have both included short stories that show the power of voice in their characters. There is a very dynamic Caribbean diasporic movement in their use of language; it is useful to note that both of these writers lived in England before emigrating to Canada.

For George Elliott Clarke, one of the Governor General's Award winners, the focus in this Collection is the historical use of the Middle Passage to engage in human trafficking. He traces the journey of the African to the New World in an epic poem. Clarke's voice in the poem is full of such energy and passion that it took my breath away in its storytelling movement and flow, and rhythm—its now and then staccato dip and trip, and the rise to a crescendo. The poem is aptly titled "A Record of the Ruction."

Other poets in the collection include: Clifton Joseph, Motion, Dwayne Morgan, Jelani Nias (J-wyze), and Mansa Trotman. Their work is focused on a vast array of issues, from jazz, to love angst and the healing of it, and other life issues. In a rare moment, Clifton Joseph's focus is on "the end of a love affair": a space usually reserved by Mansa Trotman. The collection is blessed with contributions from Dwayne Morgan, Jelani Nias, and Motion—all Toronto stalwarts of the finely tuned movement of pen over words said much more briskly by tongue. They have always made the transition seem fluid and effortless, like water rolling off a duck's back.

Dub poet Clifton Joseph is a well-known international figure in the world of dub poetry, and is also a journalist whose work has earned him two Gemini Awards. Poet Dwayne Morgan is a Harry Jerome Award winner for Excellence in the Arts. His albums of poetry recorded with music accompaniment have earned three Canadian Urban Music Awards.

Motion, Dwayne Morgan, Jelani Nias, and Mansa Trotman are poets whose work I have admired. Image-making is one of the strengths of these writers. Their work has a way of picking you up and dashing you across from where you believe you're sitting. Suddenly, you find yourself thinking in the vivid imageries that they paint.

Clearly, this gathering of African Canadian writers' fresh writings will be useful in the classroom, as well as for personal collections.

CATHERINE BAIN

One Hand Can't Clap

Betty looked around and saw her mother having a conversation with two of her friends, Janet and Medal. She knew that this was big people conversation by the whispered tones and the proximity to each other. Janet's arms were folded across her belly, overstretched from carrying the six "special gifts" that God had blessed her with. Her head leaned to the side where Ida was standing as she listened to every word that dropped from Ida's lips and intensely looked down at the parched soil as if the subject of the conversation was at her feet.

Medal, arms akimbo, had a look that was stern. Betty thought to herself, "If looks could kill, somebody would be stone cold dead." Betty's curiosity was so intense that the painting in Grandma's house called *The Rebellion* flashed across her eyes and she knew that an important secret was being shared. Common wisdom had taught her that when adult conversation was taking place you kept your distance from within earshot or a stern warning to "watch your manners" or a telling off was hurled at you. But she could measure accurately the mood of the conversation though not the content by the facial expressions and gestures from each woman. Her mother was gesturing animatedly with both hands with a staccato rhythm and she knew that she was in distress. Her eyes looked sad and her body sagged as if she had worked all day sorting nutmeg and mace, then home to a tub of dirty laundry, or a wooden tray of laundry to be ironed and delivered the next morning. Betty's stomach did a butterfly somersault and then settled down to a flutter. She must find out what was making Ma sad and nervous.

Circling the back of her house, she removed the dry laundry from the clotheslines facing the women "to catch the eyes of the judges," then slowly and methodically folded them and placed them in the tray, each article assigned to its group. She was seeking acknowledgement that she was a help to her mother. Like a dancer she wound her way to the centre rows, a place to hear but not be seen. The dance must be slowed down and removal of the laundry drawn out as a slow, dreamy musical note. She worked her way in a circle till the last empty line led her to face the judges once more. Snippets of conversation were tucked away to be pieced together later in quiet contemplation, then sewn like a patchwork quilt to unfold the story.

"It is not easy when you know that you are doing everything you can for your family, working like a slave in the nutmeg pool, coming home to a tub of laundry and a washing board or hours over a coal pot of iron and a drunken fool squandering his money and treating you like nothing. It is enough to make a saint commit a felony," said Janet. "Ida don't let that man make you lose your soul. I am praying for you day and night. I did not marry a saint either. He tries my patience every day. Lazy as spit! He likes to talk about man work and woman work. If I don't ask, it will never get done. We have to teach boys and girls to do all kinds of work and get rid of that stupidness. One thing I make clear, he must bring the pay cheque home. And I send him to pay all the bills, and keep the receipts on a wire rack he made. When he objects I remind him that Paradise Island have dishonest people and we need to protect ourselves. I am keeping my eyes on every penny to take care of our children. I tell him, 'Norbert, don't lose the key to your brain and raise your hand at me, because it will be goodbye time. You know we are here for you with whatever we can do to help.'"

Medal was still looking angry, "Phillip is another one that I have to ask him if a carpenter make his hands. I remind him to bend the elbows from time to time. But I was thinking about something. I think that women encourage the man work and woman work idea. My mother and father have their problems. Before they got married my mother told my father that she was not giving up her job in Mr. Rodman's store. She did not want children because she had to take care of eight brothers and sisters since she was six. She told him 'My children days are over. I had to fight to stay in school to complete school leaving exam and make a life for myself.' He refused to sign for a hysterectomy, so he took care of the children and the house because she was the one with carpenter-made hands. I am not saying it is right, but the point is she told him up front what she expected and he agreed to it. And guess what? All the neighbours stopped talking to her. They call her lazy, a worthless woman who take advantage of her husband, crazy, and he should get some backbone and show her who the man is. He is not a violent man and he loves my mother. But both of them are despised because they don't follow what people think is normal.

"Phillip and I share the care of the children and both of us sign for the loan to buy the house. That was my father's idea because his father was a woman beater, and his mother worked as an estate donkey and had no say in anything. He was like Rudolph, so you know that money was in their house like Christmas. When he died, Phillip and one sister paid the debt. She took over the mortgage.

"Ida, I know that you do the best you can for your family and I am not criticizing, I only making observations. Marriage is a hard thing and raising a family too. I don't have the answers. But ill treatment is wrong. If we keep on hiding it, we are letting it continue. We afraid to talk about it because we think it is our fault and we ashamed people will know. The point is they know. Who the hell like to be treated like shit? The one doing the beating is not ashamed because it is a secret. Let us know what we could do. Call me if you need me anytime."

"Thanks. You don't know how much you help me already. See you all tomorrow, please God."

Betty had heard enough and had gone on ahead of her mother to the garden at the back of the house to get provision for supper. Her brother Paul used to take care of the garden, but he had confronted his father about beating and mistreating his mother and Rudolph had asked him to leave. Paul lived with his paternal grandparents who were unhappy with their son's behaviour.

Ida joined Betty in the garden. "What we cooking tonight, Ma?"

"What you fancy, bakes and smoked herring or oil down? Don't pull up that bush; it's ven-ven and it good for rashes and cooling the blood."

"We all like oil down. You and Grandma May and Granny make the best food. Ma, you think Daddy will stop drinking?"

"I don't know. We have to continue praying for him." Ida felt helpless; she knew that her children were affected by the fear and violence. The only help she felt that could work was divine intervention. "How was school today?"

"Good. Mr. Jack got a job on the same boat his brother working on. Marilyn tell me."

"Is true?" That was news to Ida.

"You know what else? Big mouth Robert announce to the schoolyard that daddy borrow five dollars from his father and did not pay him back. He said his father told his mother that he still waiting for it after two months, so he might as well treat it as a gift."

"That man is an embarrassment to his family. He have the whole of Sea Breeze washing their mouth on us. I sorry you and your brother have to face all of that."

"You remember when Daddy used to take us to watch cricket and football, and when he used to win the Regatta Race almost every year. He wanted us to meet all his friends, tell us jokes, and bring home treats. Paul and I liked when he used to tell us Ananci stories. He was so funny; he would act them out, and we would laugh a lot. What happen to make him so nasty? Now he is always drunk, ignores us, doesn't care for Grandpa and he tells Granny lies to get her to give him money. Grandpa ban him from visiting if he is not home. He won't even give you money to pay for the land. What if we lose everything? I get so angry when I hear the nasty things he would say when you ask him for money. Paul is right; the only person he thinks about is himself. I am so frighten, Ma, that he will kill you. Tuesday night I was trembling when he slammed your head into the partition. Look at you Ma, you still wearing that head scarf. And don't tell me all family have their problems. Not all families have a drunk who bully and beat them up. We lost Paul; he said he is never coming back. I won't leave you alone. I am going to do well in school and get a good job so we can live on our own. I promise you, Ma!" The anger and rage had boiled over. Betty started to weep loudly.

Her mother ran to her and held her close, helpless tears mingling with Betty's. She felt as though she was buried under an avalanche of stones and could not breathe, "I promise you Betty, things will change." As she uttered these words she knew that she had to save herself and her children without knowing how. "Ma, promise me you won't answer back when he try to pick a quarrel."

"I promise."

In the kitchen, Betty tried to lighten the anxiety she knew that mother was also feeling. She told her about an article that she had read about American women marching and burning their bras as a symbol of rejection of their roles as nothing more than mothers, housekeepers, and wives. "There is a tablet that women are taking to prevent them from having babies if they don't want them. That is what we need here, so people won't have a lot of children that they can't take care of. That is a good thing, eh Ma? What I like best of all is, women want to get the same pay as men for doing the same work. Think of that, Ma. In the nutmeg pool you, Miss Medal, and Miss Janet getting the same money as the men. That could cause a riot in this country. That would cause a lot of men like Daddy who want to control women to go stark raving mad. It kind of scary, but it's fair. Some of the girls in class say that if you want control of your life you have to work for your own money. You work for your money and Daddy is still boss over everything we own. If I was living there I would march and make a lot of noise with those women."

Ida was outraged that women were taking the Pill as birth control. "That don't sound right to me. Children are gifts from God. I am blessed to have you and Paul. If I took that tablet I would not have had you both. But it is fair that if you work the same as a man you should get the same pay. Hell will freeze over if that happen here. Burning bras and walking around with your bubbies down to your navel or flapping around is common."

All conversation ceased as Rudolph entered with a slurred "Goodnight." A chorus of "Goodnight, Rudolph" and "Goodnight, Daddy" recited in flat tones, then silence, like a closed door, shut out speech between mother and daughter. The meal preparation continued. Words were not spoken but a dialogue between Betty and Ida was taking place. No heads were turned to look at each other, but a tension passed between mother and daughter. No visible emotion mirrored on faces but imperceptibly the message shared was that silence should prevail; stirring an ants' nest was not wise. Loud snoring broke the silence. Rudolph was asleep. The tension felt was relaxed. Supper was eaten and to bed they went, leaving Rudolph to sleep till morning on the sofa. He awakened in the early morning—before birds and their wives were awake to sing their songs to awaken men as the sun rose over the hills— and left hurriedly.

Ida met Medal and Janet outside the sorting shed, "How goes the battle, girls?" She greeted her friends. "Soldering on," they responded, which was a colloquial expression for status quo.

"We had a peaceful night. The Boss Man slept the sleep of the drunk. I had an interesting conversation with Betty," and she related the conversation. The reaction was mixed. Bernice thought that birth control was interference with God's plan. She shared her birth control method with her friends. She slept in the girls' room although this made Norbert unhappy. There were benefits, however. Norbert helped in the house without being asked and gave her more attention. Medal was excited about women demanding financial equality, but the conversation had to be stopped as work was about to begin. They decided to pursue the conversation at lunch.

At lunch the workers sat on benches outside or under trees eating, gossiping or teasing, or sharing their life's stories with each other. It was difficult to keep one's life private, living in such close proximity. Before the morning conversation could be continued, a group sitting close by started gossiping about a young, pretty woman who had emigrated from Trinidad to Sea Breeze. The "brango" or gossip was that she was Skipper's girlfriend and was sent to take care of her sick aunt. "Nothing is wrong with Mona; she is hale and hearty. You did see her in the New Year's dance, dancing up and eying all the good looking men. I think Edith mother send her here to cool off some of the fire running wild in she blood."

Teresita, another queen of gossip, chirped in: "Well it look like Rudolph is the fireman outing the fire." Loud laughter erupted with little regard for Ida who overheard every word but was pretending to be deaf. She knew that the gossip was true, but was fighting to keep her head above water for her children's sake. Medal led the group to another bench away from the laughing women. The bell sounded for their return to work, a welcome relief.

The walk home at the end of the day was subdued. The conversation started in the morning was postponed for now. The friends feeling keenly Ida's sadness and helplessness walked in silent companionship with her, encouraging her to "Keep your chin up."

The evening routine at Ida's house with Betty and her sharing chores and conversation went on as usual. They smelled him before he entered the door. The perfume of rum was wafting on the air. He stumbled to the Morris chair. "Good evening, Daddy." He slurred a response. All further discussion ceased, and the task of cooking was resumed in silence. Their silent, unemotional conversation was learned through observation and sensitivity to emotions. No looking in the eyes, no heads turned, but imperceptively the warning given by that silence was demanded. Disturbing the serpent was not wise.

"Ida, come here. Mr. Brown, the boss at the bank, say that we owe two months on the land. You were supposed to be paying every month because you know I have some debt to pay back. So when they throw us off the land don't blame me. You are working two jobs so you should be paying the bills. If you can't take responsibilities for that one thing give the money to me and I will pay it tomorrow. You are useless as always. Why I saddle myself to you I will never know. Oh yes, I know. You tricked me into getting you pregnant. You trying to get me to take all the responsibility for this family, eh? Well I am not a millionaire yet, so you have to pay that bill. Better still: give me the money when you get your paid tomorrow. You understand?"

She had promised Betty not to answer and cause Rudolph to lose his temper. She had enough of his constant irresponsible behaviour and blaming it on her. Enough of his disrespectful way of speaking to her and treating her and the children as invisible objects. There was no thank you for the extra efforts to keep the family together by shouldering all the responsibilities. She had given him power over her and the children and it had caused her son to leave and her daughter to become her protector rather than the other way around. This must stop. The conversation in her head continued. "I am sick and tired being afraid for the children and myself. I am ashamed for letting him do this us. I was too weak to protect Paul; I will not let you chase Betty away, no more beatings. I am a good person, but you make me doubt that I am capable."

She took a deep breath to suppress the raging sea of anger within her, looked him in the eye (something that she had not done for many years) and remembered that his eyes were brown. "I once loved those eyes," she thought. She spoke slowly, "Rudolph are you my husband or am I your slave and you the master? Answer me!" Her voice rose and fell like a wave signalling a coming storm. "I have endured your insults, your beatings, kicking, pushing, and forcing yourself on me. You told Dr. Brown that I slipped in the land and lost the baby. I was too ashamed to say that you kicked it out of me. It stops tonight! Betty, go to Medal next door." Gently and reassuringly she spoke to Betty, who saw the terror in her eyes. "Go. I will be okay." Betty, thinking her ma had gone mad, ran up the hill to get Medal. Her body was shaking like a loose leaf readying to loosen its hold on a tree.

"Woman, what did you just say to me?" He bellowed. He tried to get up quickly and stumbled backward sprawling onto the sofa. "Answer me," he slurred. "I will show you who the master is!" Making an effort to rise again and lifting his fist in a menacing way, he got up. Lifting a chair he threw it at her head. She anticipated this and pulled away from the path of the missile. His eyes were full of rage as he made a stumbling but determined path towards her. She did not shift her steely gaze from his face. Dodging obstacles in her way she was steering herself backwards towards the door where the machete stood like a sentinel in the corner. He became the hunter and she his prey. Not a sound she uttered, nothing felt but the urgency of freedom pushing her along. Rudolph feeling the rage of his fragile ego waning summoned his strength to subdue his prey. Her hand felt the object of her desire. She held it tightly and raised her hand slowly; she was ready for the flight to freedom. All was lost in and around her except the face of the hunter and the hard metal in her right hand. Slowly, she lifted the blade in the air leaning slowly backward like a graceful dancer. A loud booming voice caused her to stumble and stay her hand, "Stop."

Rudolph was gone from her life. Fear made him take flight for preservation of life like she did that night. She had found her voice, hoarse and hesitant from lying dormant, but slowly she learned to know and appreciate it. But scars too deep to be touched with soothing balm remained, scabbed over but unhealed. Life's rough edges would cause the pain again. Freedom for Ida wore two faces like Janus. She struggled to keep moving forward, listening to her voice, but the distant whisper of her past would pop up like a blackbird in the mango tree. She would repeat her mantra and keep moving one step at a time. "I am a good person."

Catherine Bain has been a nurse for thirty-nine years. She is passionate about nursing, and sees it as an honour to be of service to patients and their families during challenging periods in their lives. She was a teacher in Grenada before emigrating to England. She says of her writing: "I have been writing since I was a teenager; I was spurred on by a friend's unconditional love, and by the love of books and stories. My writing is influenced by having grown up in a culture of colonial social inequalities, and narrow social and political norms. My work as a mental health nurse has also influenced my writing. I seek to find the human strength in challenging situations and the responsibility of society."

GEORGE ELLIOTT CLARKE

A Record of the Ruction

Whips clawed our backs daily.

Clammy, milky, stinking pirates
took our mothers as spreadable honey and legs.

Surf dumped foam on the blazing beach
when we staggered onto the slaver,
reeking from weak bladders and fright,
a piss aroma.

The beach (African) was snow-white sand.
Surf came pure cream,
milk-silk-milk.
And beyond that foam-combed margin,
swam a white-green, spearmint,
then a forest-green,
then a blue-green,
and still farther out, at the horizon,
planed a pale plain,
and beyond that too,
veering to th'Americas,
a periwinkle-tinctured pink.

En route to that cream shore,
defiled through jungles,
the sick among us got fed,
laughingly, to crocs;
others were blasted through the kneecap
and left, screaming, for hyenas.

On the beach—
the churn of waves at sand,
blushing with bloodshed and damage—
proved the fervent carnage
unleashed by ruddy "tars"—
vassals of a hemophiliac imperialism….
Their work was lashing, hacking, cutting away at us,
hollering, "Don't let the livestock
stray like fish,"
as their vessels
lay fallow in the shoals,
and crows—vultures—drifted serenely above
this bloodbath globe.

New ropes bit into old limbs.

The vulture-chartered sky oversaw
monsters who take, break, choke, and chew.
They fondle coins; they manhandle gold.

Howls rolled about us like balls-and-chains
as one "Jolly Roger" and the next
used our Guinea beauties like white wantons,
delivering hot, crowding thrusts,
even snidely stabbing at times.

The *baas* man, Captain,
havocked my Queen in his hammock;
she revoked herself,
broke seawater, and sank.
Her piling tears dissolved
into aqua-blue silence.

I felt my soul put to death.

Hatred swamped my heart;
Wrath drove hot bile through my veins.

The crew connived at *Lechery*,
held down each fat *femme*,
fucked maiden, *mère,* and grandmother,
like maggots drilling into meat.

Coarse sweat in dusty sheets,
some sooty, *sotto voce* vice.

(Redeem the violators?
Say rum is their salvation,
wine their solution;
say each one downs a gallon of ale.
Say each one interprets freely
his own costly bottle.

I agree:
Your compatriots—The Devil's Christians—
plugged themselves up with liquor,
then dragged down proud mammies, proud babes....

Thus, each pallid malefactor merited
being flung down in fluid darkness.

Note:
Your kings, clergy, and clerks bless *Slavery*.
For you, the sun is the hot gold coin
at a wench's thighs;
the moon is a cool, half-dollar
in the night's black fist.
Your horsefly preaching insists,
"Shit is good!"

But, as God is my witness,
you and yours are nonchalant killers.

So be it.

All histories have their routes.
Darkness wakens light.

Terror
resolves *Error.*)

Aboard *Evil*'s vessel, I told myself
"It's only a toy, this ship."
I calculated my ascension to command,
to break bigots
down to maggots.

Our Babel'd whispers slapped like whips
about the hold.

But some of us caught meaning like a sting.

I swore I'd be self-freed.
(I'd sooner nourish the gallows
than ever the auction block.)

(Now I know in Haiti, the machete
outvoted a king
and armed an ex-slave Republic
not even Napoleon could seize.)

Spirited conspiracy
inspired our "piracy."

Our gruel was unbecoming, watery tea;
our soup looked like the glittering, turgid spew
of your sewers.

You've tutored me to appreciate
the hopeless chaos of *Liberation*—
by steel and fire and sharp glass.

We swore
to be the worse,
reckless
killers.

(Albicide shadows negricide.)

Sailors—slavers—had crept among our chains,
next night and the next,
to rive more of our wives,
whose screams they stifled
with pink-lipped slobbers.

For you *toubab*, each "I" heads up an "it,"
a thing, inhuman, a *unit*.

"Providently"
(as your preachers would have it),
a single loose nail rolled by my pen,
and I made it a gouge

to churn the wood round the square-shanked nails
clinching my chains to the deck;
made it a crowbar
to pry up further nails;
until I, disciple of X—
Xango—
God of iron and iron works,
felt a hushing shiver shake me
as my shackles clinked free.

An iron-coloured man with a mind set in stone,
exercising chessboard plotting but a boxer's speed,
I wrested free my restless brother,
then unchained our restless brethren,

to muster "treachery,"

not a second too-hasty,

given the unmitigated scarcity of water,
our blinding hunger
(our ribs felt naked within),

also the memory of "blackamoor" heads them "buckaroos"
posted
atop the stockade's fence on our beach,
and their degradation of bronze dames and daughters,
and their outrages against God and humanity,
well....

*   *   *   *

Here is a stormy chronicle—
a gale-force history
I regale you with:
Genesis begins with Exodus....

According to your Bard, W.S.,
at the verge of gore,
atmospheric and oceanic tempers
whip forth tempests:
lightning's crucified pon the night
whenever a god's to be crossed.

Hence, God sends bursts of light
from dawning dark.

The ship broaches crippling weather.
Waves pump up, plump,
then tumble, crumbling into surf.
A storm distresses and stutters our planks.
Lightning marries—and divorces—the night.

We slink through our own manure
in panther-smooth manoeuvres.

We scrunch up, sneak about,
collect every bit of glass
or metal,
even chains, even the loosened nails.

Each of us creeps on top—
as stealthy as assassins—

into cold, blizzarding rain,
the night one surging swell,
creamy rage,
rigging a-squeak, sails squawking,
rickety howling clamour
whickering and hammering about
in melodrama as horrible as your Bible plagues.

We witness a hither-and-slithering sea,
here-and-there crests,
a devouring void—
indiscernible sky,
charcoal tempest.

Clouds chop down the stars;
rain chops up the sea.

We "tarred" men tarry not,
but infiltrate the pitch and ooze of the eve.

When some of our captors see us,
they are kneeling,
praying—most assuredly—to Satan.

My command? "Let em heave out hymns
while we heave em overboard.

"Let their sobs pelt into the vast wet!"

Now we surge up against pointed rifles,
snow-faced men who make coffins
as quickly as they make coffee,
but we stomp down the insects,
sink steel or sharp glass
into 99% of the whites.

Scum, roaches, shit, shipboard-ruddying blows,
our dead—slain—children, blood, girls ripped open,
all urged along our placid murdering.

Our blades glide,
glistering like blistering light.

No stray tenderness hinders
our supple movements
mid the rippling darkness.

We are as bloodless in our massacre art
as strategic thinkers in your universities.

A terrific tantrum!
A cyclone of slashings!
While rain sprouts on our faces,
blood spurts from their blanching bellies.

Through night's pitchy horror,
our fists bluster;

knives and sharp glass
show mettle and lustre,

cankering flour-coloured flesh
to so much ruddy custard.

(Each damp puncture
hooks a fishy wound.)

The Europeans, once bestial with ale,
now beleaguered, ailing,
show a bloody blot—

as our jagged bottles, ragged blades,
whipping chains, ripped-up floor nails,

churn their sorry faces
into too-ripe, burst-open peaches.

We do business
with calipers stuck through necks,
grapples hooked in bellies,
canvas needles,
harpoons,
marlin spikes,

chisels,
caulking irons,
pointed-ended rasps,
punches,
cutlasses,
kitchen knives,
and, yes, broad axes.

Insidious bliss drives on our dicing.
The dead topple down with looks
as enigmatic as playing-card royalty.

Each cleavered visage
spews toxic materials—
gore, blubber, slime, tears, snot....

Each bit of bloodshed soothes
blisters and abrasions their chains caused us.

When I trap Captain Septimus Optimus,
he's sunk in rum and a black gal's sex,
and he knows he's as doomed as Hamlet,
père et fils.

The fat-bellied fucker stands,
as wobbly as water,
still groggy from drink—
his manhood dripping, soggy—

and I hit him with a two-edged meat cleaver:
He looked like egg white flayed by a whisk.

He cries and foams a meringue.
but his wound cleaves to my cleaving knife.

I feel no greater liberty
than when my blade skewers his guts.

Cap's hapless scalping
shows off his brains
as a luminous wound.

Happily, I toss Optimus—that rubbish—out,
watch him plunge fathoms down
in murky grunge.

Returning to the fury without,
the black expanse of rain,
I see the dying crew's scattered agony,
the lithe writhing of some,
all composing unpaintably delicious pain,

and I bid my unchained men
jettison the bloody debris
to make sharks merry—

and revenge those of us thrown
from skiffs and scows
as croc food.

We leave alive only one of em—
the pilot—
basically, "Judas"—
to shepherd us to Africa.
Aye, we chain him to the wheel.

Strangely, after our prickling and pinking
of the naval devils,
the sea softens to a warm silver,
the opened rum kegs waft a buttery scent,
and we and our living allies dance,
giddy with fresh mobility.

After our work,
we have wine, rum,
and waltz amid wet air.

Fatigued, but glorious,
I swing swigs of sinuous rum.

Leprous stars, blanched, pale as fog,
a-between cloud strands.

As dawn shows,
shadows cascade in,
slide behind us with the waxing light.

Wan waves wane—
chromatic grey—
as the horizon cuts down distance.

An ashy dawn,
a rumpled white sea.

We pass from Turner's *The Slave Ship*
to his canvas, *The Burning of the Houses of Parliament.*

Columns of light support marble clouds—
amid glinting spray.

Next, the mist, sun-incinerated,
turns phosphorescent, albescent.

First, only pitiful light sifts the vague fog;
vigilant, our silhouettes await brilliantined light.

At last, sunlight emerges
as vivid as a white bitch's wet cunt.

Behold the Atlantic's abundant glitter!

Our freed ship, turned derelict,
drifts in an invisible maze,
pristinely walled, floored, and ceilinged by light.

The sun again makes spacious the sky.

*   *   *   *

Delirious liberty
became our own as we rode
the sea's undulant irregularities,
and we became more-and-more short on water,
but ever big on rum.

With one-eyed accuracy,
unerring cunning,
the spared pilot, Judas,
swung us by night—
and by shady-looking daylight—
nearer and nearer to your Republic,
Land of (Ltd.) Liberty.

Our wheelman's direction was zigzag,
as skittish as a mosquito.

Then, running under a grey sky
with a peek-a-boo sun—
or a cloud-squished, cloud-squashed sun—

one of your Coast Guard cutters
loomed from mist-gloom,
and, spying us out to be all black but one,
figured we'd had a revolution,
and cannon'd us to a halt.

Custodying us like a slave shipment,
the Yankee sailors promised us
the charismatic halo of a noose
as soon as our toes touched beach.

So what?

I'd don a rope,
Having thrown off chains.

Reaching these awful provinces—
your by-laws of hangings and beheadings—
I saw waves launch froth at boulders,
the ocean's fangs viper this coast.

Since then, I've faced,
via torturous scrutiny,
judgments disgraced,
accusing me of mutiny.

The rest you know.
History smoulders upon the pyres
of empires.

Your own republican courts—
despite guaranteeing *Slavery*—
recognized our hard-won suzerainty,
acclaiming it as you had claimed yours.

Free—
at last, again, free—

my wish is to roam,
then moor,
led by the God of Rome—
(unlike Aaron the Moor)—

unto the landfall of light—

unforeseen light—
out of unexpected darkness.

My panther anthem?

Liberty! Beauty! Justice!

Jesus Caesar
(*alias* Boukman)
Washington, D.C.
1815

Corpus Christi (Texas) 17 avril mmviii

Photo by Camelia Linta

George Elliott Clarke (1960-) hails from Windsor, Nova Scotia, and is the inaugural E.J. Pratt (Poet) Professor of Canadian Literature at the University of Toronto. A prizewinning poet and novelist, Clarke is also revered for his plays, opera libretti, and literary scholarship. His honours include The Archibald Lampman Award for Poetry (1991), The Portia White Prize for Artistic Excellence (1998), a Bellagio Center (Italy) Fellowship (1998), The Governor General's Literary Award for Poetry (2001), The Dr. Martin Luther King, Jr. Achievement Award (2004), The Pierre Elliott Trudeau Fellowship Prize (2005–08), The Premiul Poesis (Romania) (2005), The Dartmouth Book Award for Fiction (2006), and The Eric Hoffer Book

Award for Poetry (2009). Clarke also holds eight honorary doctorates. His major titles include *Whylah Falls* (1990), *Beatrice Chancy* (1999), *Execution Poems* (2000), *George & Rue* (2005), *Blues and Bliss: The Poetry of George Elliott Clarke*, ed. Jon Paul Fiorentino (2008), and a landmark volume of literary criticism, *Odysseys Home: Mapping African-Canadian Literature* (2002). His current project is an epic poem, "Canticles," treating the era of transatlantic slavery and the attendant debates. "A Record of the Ruction" is from that manuscript-in-progress.

GAYLE GONSALVES

A Good Woman

Seven years ago, Linden hastily packed his belongings and moved to Toronto, a city that is vastly different from his small island Caribbean roots, where he thrives in the varying weather patterns. During the frigid winter period, he finds solace in books. And on bright summer days, he makes his way to the shores of Lake Ontario where its immense, sparkling brilliance reminds him of the Caribbean Sea. He closes his eyes and imagines being on a beach with Sandra; her mahogany skin glistens in the water; she delicately picks up a shell from the sand; she smiles as she shows him the perfectly shaped shell. Her beautiful, slender fingers touch his arm, moving with the same grace and tenderness she does when she paints a canvas.

....

It is through the small island grapevine in Toronto that Linden hears about Auntie Jeannie's illness and he's desperate to know what's going on. With extreme trepidation he calls Antigua, and Sandra answers the phone. Her voice is still a magical, musical tone, and he can't help but melt as she speaks. For a moment, he drifts into his fantasyland, but is pulled back to reality when she tells him if he wants to see his aunt one final time, he'd better come home soon.

"I'll take the first flight I can get," he tells her.

"Good," she says. Then she adds, "You know you can't stay here. Kelvin won't have it."

"No problem," he replies, flustered and embarrassed. "I'll make arrangements for a hotel."

Two weeks later, he's asking her a question that upsets her, "Do you think Kelvin's going to make it to Auntie Jeannie's funeral?"

Sandra turns to Linden as he speaks. He looks into her luminous, brown eyes. For a moment, she lets down her defences and returns his gaze. They are alone in her home, surrounded by the bright canvases she paints, no one can disturb them, yet when he reaches for her, she turns away.

"He can't live in the rum shop forever. It'll kill him," Sandra quickly replies. "It must be Auntie Jeannie's death that sent him over the edge."

Shortly after they speak, Sandra leaves Linden and takes a short stroll. She walks for a while and then eventually finds herself on Vivian Richards Street and she makes her way along the narrow thoroughfare to the rum shop. From the road, she hears dominoes slamming on a table and the boisterous voices of the men as they discuss the "tiefing" or "holiness" of the government. The rusted, worn-out sign, *Rawle's, a p ace for fri nds,* hangs lopsided; one of its screws fell a few years ago. The strong smell of the alcohol repulses her but she ignores it as she opens the shoddy, wooden door that leads to Rawle's. She quickly surveys the room and finds Kelvin in his usual corner spot.

She touches his hand, "Kelvin, come nuh, tomorrow we bury Auntie Jeannie and you need to clean up. You've had enough. It's time to come home."

He looks up from his glass with glazed eyes and slurs, "Sssssssannnnnndrrrraaa, darllllinggg, me one true love. Me can't leave yyyettt. Be a goooooddd wiiffee and jjjussttt sit with mmmeee wwwwhilllllle me gggoooo have one for de rrrooaddddd."

"Kelvin, the bottle goin' kill you. It's time to stop." But he ignores her and pours himself a drink. She shakes her head in disgust and leaves him sitting on the hard barstool.

Sandra walks slowly on the cracked concrete sidewalk, carefully navigating the holes and cracks. The route home is different as she leaves the familiar streets of her neighbourhood and walks north, past Country Pond and through town until she's in a new area where there are homes with beautiful flowers. Her eyes take everything in. She looks at several houses and then she stops in front of a quaint, green house with a small hedge of yellow bells, and a yard filled with pawpaw trees. Her artistic eyes admire its lines and dimensions. And she looks at it for a long time before she makes her long return trek. Once home, she sits on the couch and looks blankly at the walls that are filled with her beautiful artwork. And she spends all night looking at them.

On the following day, Sandra dresses in a black frock and attends Auntie Jeannie's funeral with Linden. Her legs shake as she walks next to the casket. She sobs uncontrollably and Linden holds her tenderly during the funeral. He's surprised by her grief but he's acutely aware that Sandra is in a very emotional state. After the funeral, she stares at the walls of the house that are filled with her paintings. He watches her warily as she touches her paintbrush and then violently throws it to the ground.

"Let's get out of here," he says as he tugs her arm, fearful that she could cause some damage. "You need to get away. I've been home for nearly a week and haven't been to the sea. I think it's calling us."

Twenty minutes later, he and Sandra are making their way to Fort James Beach, driving on the island's familiar, narrow roads and masterfully swerving potholes. Although neither of them can see the beach, they smell the salt in the air and hear the hypnotic sound of the water breaking at the shore. When they finally see the brilliant aqua waters blend into the horizon, their eyes dance with joy. As soon as he turns off the ignition, Linden hears the car door open and before he can say anything, he sees Sandra hastily run from the car and spontaneously jump into the water. Her gleeful screams fill the air as her body hits the water and makes Linden smile. He instinctively runs into the water to be with her. On that afternoon, he falls in love with her again as the clock moves backward and forward. Together they walk on the sand. Sandra picks up shells and when she sees one that intrigues her, he listens carefully as she talks about its colour and lines. He is comforted that she is still the Sandra he remembers and he wants so desperately for her to be happy. They leave when the sun sets. That evening, she doesn't think about her husband who is wasting away at Rawle's. Instead, she returns to her canvas and paints the shell. And she surprises Linden by painting a quaint green house surrounded by yellow bells. He notices that her colours are bright; her colours are vibrant; and she's smiling.

Linden and Kelvin are brothers. When their father was alive, he'd say, "How can two pickney from the same belly be so different?"

Throughout their entire lives, everyone who met them commented on their differences. Kelvin, with his dark, athletic looks, was well-known for his wild spirit. He drank, partied and when he entered a room in a tight t-shirt that accentuated his perfect physique, he'd yell, "Whoa! Whoa! Whoa! Kelvin is here! Bring the rum, bring the coke. Start the music." Linden, on the other hand, was the epitome of sophistication. Always immaculately dressed, he preferred crisp, well-pressed pin-striped shirts with a starched collar to t-shirts. While his brother enjoyed laughing in a crowd, Linden favoured a good book and didn't waste his time on inane social chatter. Kelvin, the entrepreneur of the two, barely passed school but owned a small business that provided for him and his wife. Linden, the scholar, enjoyed analyzing social behaviour and actions. He pursued post-secondary education and commanded a very decent wage at the bank. Only a year apart, the only thing they had in common was their love for Sandra.

After he finished school, Linden won a scholarship to university and left Antigua for several years. During his absence, his brother shocked his family, friends, and all the gossipers on the island, by pursuing and marrying the thoughtful and artistic Sandra. For a short time after he placed the wedding ring on her finger, he quietened down and those who knew him believed that he'd left his wild ways behind him.

When Linden returned to the island, Kelvin was already spending more time at Rawle's than with his wife. His business was suffering and he asked his brother to move in with them to help with the bills. Linden agreed. Kelvin was pleased with the arrangement; he felt reassured that his brother would make sure no man was "horning" him. But Kelvin never knew or suspected that Linden was obsessed with Sandra's luminous eyes and deep copper complexion.

Every night, Kelvin kissed his wife delicately on the cheek, "I'm just going up the road with the boys. I'll be home later."

As the door closed behind him, Linden quietly smiled because he was alone with Sandra. There, under the roof they all shared, Linden's infatuation grew into love as he discovered Sandra's calm, creative nature. Each night, out of the corner of his eyes, he watched Sandra with absolute fascination. He loved the way she twisted her hair into a scarf before she began painting. He was wholly intrigued with her slender fingers and how they nimbly worked the paintbrush as she created new lines and shapes. As Kelvin disappeared more and more, Sandra and Linden spent a lot of time together. Once Kelvin used to go with his wife every Saturday afternoon to the beach but his brother took his place. Together, Linden and Sandra swam in the crystal clear waters and laughed. He'd watch Sandra scour for shells, and when she found one that met her approval, she'd show it to Linden. Her fingers traced its lines as she told him about its texture, dimension, and colour. He loved getting a glimpse into her world and seeing objects through her eyes.

And one Saturday evening, after they returned from the beach, with the sand clinging to their bodies,

Linden gave into his desires and pulled Sandra to him. He kissed her on the lips and was ecstatic when her lips moved with his. Then, she pulled away, "I can't. This isn't right."

"Leave him," Linden pleaded. "Marry me. We can make a life together. He doesn't deserve someone as good as you."

"This is crazy. I'm married to your brother. How did this happen?"

"Stop thinking and let it be."

"Linden, this is madness. Utter madness. I'm married to your brother."

"Sandra, I don't care. He doesn't deserve you. Love has no rules."

"He's not all bad. I know the Kelvin few ever see." She paused, "Rum is not a good thing." And she left the room.

The following night, Linden noticed that Sandra was looking at him through the corner of her eyes and waited impatiently for Kelvin to leave. As soon as he closed the door, Linden pulled her into his arms. This time she didn't protest. And finally she opened up to Linden.

"This is not easy, you know. I thought about what you said. It's not like I don't have feelings for you. I do." Linden's heart beat fast as she spoke, "If I'd met you before I met Kelvin this would be so different but I didn't. You are his brother and this isn't right."

Linden didn't hear the last part of her sentence and he responded impulsively, "Let's go away together. My papers for Canada just came in. Join me. Divorce him and marry me. I promise that I'll honour and..."

Kelvin's hand connected with Linden's jaw and he didn't finish his sentence. On that night, Kelvin forgot his wallet and returned home to overhear his brother asking his wife to run away with him. Without thinking, he threw his fist at Linden's jaw then continued to attack him. Linden tasted his blood and tried to shield himself from his brother's blows but couldn't stop the assault. Horrified, Sandra threw her body between the brothers.

"Stop this," she screamed frantically. "Just stop this. Don't do this. Please, don't do this. One of you might kill the other."

"What do you expect? My brother is trying to 'tief' my wife."

The two brothers glared at each other. Linden wiped the blood from his nose, "You don't deserve her. She's a good woman and all you do is drink and party. I love Sandra."

Sandra frantically grabbed and held Kelvin with all her strength as he lurched at Linden, "I'm goin to kill you, I'm goin to kill you if you don't leave now."

Linden, genuinely fearful of the threat, quickly ran out the door. Kelvin never left his wife's side that night, truly worried that she'd run away with his brother. Over the next few days, they were like newlyweds as they rekindled their love with outings at the beach and nights of heated lovemaking. The rum left his body and Sandra remembered the man she first loved. But, after a few weeks in her company, he missed the boisterous frivolity of the rum shop. As soon as he heard that Linden was on a plane to Toronto, Kelvin kissed his wife on her lips, "I'm just going down the road to Rawle's. I won't be long."

She didn't see him until the next morning when he drunkenly returned home. And he found his way back to Rawle's the following day and every day after that. Her canvases became her company again and she spent her time painting beach scenes as she remembered her afternoons with Linden. As the years passed, her husband spent more time at Rawle's and she was left with memories of happier times. Her paintings became darker as she avoided using reds, oranges, and pinks.

On the day that Linden arrives in Antigua after his long absence, Kelvin tells Sandra, "Me nah pick him up from the airport. Let him find his way to the hotel. I still can't stomach him." Then he leaves for Rawle's. After having a few drinks, he calls his wife from the rum shop, "I'll pick up Linden at the airport and take him to the hotel. He's my brother and we need to make peace."

Linden is totally shocked when he hears his brother's familiar voice calling him when he clears customs. They eye each other warily but don't embrace; they are polite as they walk to the car, and Linden quickly notices that Kelvin stinks of rum. They leave the airport and Linden sees the brightly coloured houses that adorn the hillsides, a scene so different to the nondescript glass towers of Toronto. He tries to relax but can't.

It was Kelvin who broke the uncomfortable silence, "We need a drink before I take you to the hotel. And it's time that you and I are man enough to clear the air."

And that's how they ended up at Rawle's. The rum shop is still dingy and Linden tries not to twist his face with disdain. He gingerly takes a seat at a broken down table while Kelvin smiles in amusement at his brother's awkwardness. Before they begin to speak, Kelvin's cellphone rings.

He looks at the phone number on the display, "It's Sandra. That woman can't leave me alone, always wanting something."

His brother asks, "Shouldn't you answer it? She must be wondering where you are? Something could have happened to Auntie Jeannie."

"Believe me, nothing is the matter. When I left, Auntie was still breathing. It's Sandra keeping a tight rein on me. You know how women stop."

Linden doesn't feel comfortable, "Let's go and see

Auntie Jeannie and Sandra first. Then we can come back. I think that's better."

"I know you still love my wife after all these years," Kelvin calmly states as he looks him directly in the eye. Then his voice rises, he slams his hands on the table and everyone in the rum shop turns to look at them, "You think I forget! How can a brother do that to his brother? It's a good thing that Sandra is such a good woman. She will stay with me through thick and thin."

"Kelvin, can't we put this behind us? That's an old time story."

"No, it's not. I think you can't wait to see her again."

The phone rings again. Kelvin sees it's Sandra; again he ignores it.

"I'll call her when I'm good and ready. First, you and I need to have some words."

Kelvin orders drinks. As they arrive, he quickly drinks his and orders another. He is now quite inebriated and notices that Linden hasn't touched his glass. "What happened? You get soft living in Canada? Can't you have a drink with your brother?"

Linden takes a sip and the alcohol enters his system. His head spins. Kelvin chuckles, "Now I know you get soft. It's cause you living in that cold place you forget how to drink."

The phone rings again; Kelvin lets out a big

chupps, "This woman loves to nag me when me a drink me rum. You'd think that after all these years she know to leave me alone, nuh."

"Don't you think it could be important?"

"It someting stupid like the toilet block up."

"Then, let me answer. If it was my wife, I'd answer."

Linden tries to grab the phone from Kelvin but, even though he is drunk, Kelvin has his wits about him and grabs his brother's arm. "Nah answer my phone. Let me tell you dis, you can only speak to my wife when me say so."

"Look, I'm sorry for what I said and did years ago," Linden stutters uncomfortably, "Can't you leave it at that? You and Sandra are still together. Let it go, Kelvin. Let it go. I'm not here to mash up your marriage. I'm here to see Auntie Jeannie."

The brothers look at each other; they know they need to make a truce. Kelvin looks at him warily, "Dat better be de only reason that you come. Touch me wife and me go kill you. Sandra is a good woman. You know, when Auntie take in, Sandra tell her come live with us and she look after her like she her own mother. A man can't ask for a better wife."

Just as Kelvin speaks his last word, Linden hears her voice. He closes his eyes, desperately hoping that Kelvin doesn't notice his excitement.

"Why aren't you answering the phone, Kelvin?"

Sandra yells. "I'm so tired of you and all of this!"

He opens them, Sandra is still as beautiful and majestic as he remembers and he quietly sighs with deep longing. But Sandra and Kelvin are so caught up in their argument that they don't notice Linden.

"I knew you'd be here cause this is where you always are," she says with disgust. "Why didn't you answer the phone? You know your aunt is sick. Why, why, why do you choose to do these things? Auntie Jeannie just had a heart attack. She's in the hospital. They don't know how long she's going to last."

Kelvin looks stunned, "Are you serious?"

"You heard me. Auntie Jeannie is in the hospital. We'd better go before she dead."

The three of them hurriedly make their way to the hospital and once Auntie Jeannie sees Linden, she smiles and takes her last breath. Kelvin looks at his dead aunt and tells his wife, "I need some fresh air." He leaves and returns to Rawle's where he takes a seat on his favourite corner stool. The bartender pours him a drink. Then he refills it and Kelvin motions for him to put the bottle in front of him. Kelvin forgets about going home. And he misses his aunt's funeral.

Dogs sit outside the shop; flies cling to their mangy coats and buzz around their noses; they lie at the bottom of the steps, either too lazy or too malnourished to be bothered by the flies. Sandra is sitting in her car looking at Rawle's, remembering all the events of the past week. She hates that she has to go inside and drag Kelvin from this decrepit place. She quickly tallies the years she's spent with him and the number of times she's saved him from killing himself with a bottle of rum.

When she enters the rum shop, the men stop banging dominoes on the worn tables. The loud voices that are arguing politics and calypso music are hushed as the men look at her. They all know she's Kelvin's wife and over the years, they've seen her come and fetch him many times. They say nothing but turn their heads towards Kelvin and she follows their eyes to her husband. He's still sitting at the back of the room on an old stool. It looks hard; the wood is rotten; there is no cushion. She wonders how Kelvin can make such an uncomfortable place his home. A bottle of rum sits in front of him. His head lies heavily on the bar and she isn't sure if he's asleep or passed out.

On his face there is a scraggly beard; his body appears to be covered with a film of dirt, causing him to look like a beggar; and his body odour is foul and stale from a week of not bathing. When he hears the dominoes and chatter stop, Kelvin looks up for a moment with a dazed expression, thinking it is some man's woman or child making a scene about his absence at home. He sees Sandra; he gives her a lopsided smile.

"You miss ya maannn, Sandrrrraaaa?" he asks. She grimaces as she smells the week of alcohol on his breath. "Mmmeee always knnooow yyyouuu gggooo commmme for mmmme."

"Kelvin, shut up."

"Sandrrrraaaa, if you're notttt niccce me nah commmme hoooommme with you."

She shakes her head in disbelief. "Are you planning to kill yourself in a bottle of rum this time?"

Sandra instinctively grabs the bottle of rum that sits in front of Kelvin. Despite his intoxicated state, he's quick and also grabs it. They both hold the bottle and tug and pull at it like it's a piece of gold. Neither of them is certain whose grip lightens, if it's Kelvin's or Sandra's but when it does, the bottle falls to the ground and breaks. The liquid seeps through the cracks in the wooden floor and melts into the earth; the strong smell of alcohol permeates the room. They stare at the broken shards for a long time.

"Llllloookk aatttt what you dddiiiddd," Kelvin says.

"Kelvin, I don't have time for this crap. Do you see what you're doing to yourself? I'm so tired of this. I'm leaving." Sandra walks away.

He speaks in a whisper that's so low that Sandra barely hears him. "Ssssannndddrrraa, nnnnnnaaahhh lllleavvvveeee me here. Mmmeee go die wwwithout you."

She stops walking and turns around. He doesn't

look away. His eyes tell her the words she heard from his lips. She remembers the man that she knows he can be. This weakens her resolve and she takes his hand. She pulls him from the hard stool. Her feet are heavy as she walks to the car. His hands feel cold in hers. He hangs his head low; they don't speak.

She drives quickly to their house, afraid that if she slows down she'll change her mind. Although she is tall and strong, it takes all of her energy to pull him into the house. He stumbles on a large object as they walk through the door.

"Whattt'sss dddatttt?" he asks.

"It's nothing. I just moved some furniture," she hurriedly replies.

"Mmmmovvveeee it, sssomeoneeee ggoo get hh-hhurtttt."

"As soon as I have you settled in, I'll move it."

She takes a comb and tugs at the knots until his hair untangles. The razor slides smoothly along the grooves on his face; the week old stubble falls to the ground. He looks blankly at her as she sweeps it away. Her husband is now an infant and she helps him undress and then bathes him; layers of dirt wash down the drain. She takes the towel from the rack and dries his wet body.

He's afraid to look her in the eye and stands next to her with his head bowed, like a forlorn, repentant child. She takes his hand and leads him to their bedroom. He slumps onto the bed and pulls her down with him. He quickly falls into a deep slumber.

She's awake. The air in the house is changed. It feels darker and even though the curtains are drawn, the sun doesn't shine in the room. Kelvin sleeps. His drunken snores tells the house that he's home.

Kelvin holds her as he sleeps. His hands lie on her stomach, reminding her that he's still her husband. Once she craved that touch but now his hands feel like a heavy object pinning her down. She is uncomfortable with this closeness as she remembers they haven't been intimate in a very long time because his rum habits took precedence over her.

While he sleeps, she gets up and makes a call. She quietly whispers on the phone so he doesn't hear her. Then she hears Kelvin calling her name and she quickly puts down the receiver.

"Sandra," he yells from the other room. "Where are you, my wife? Where are you?"

She stands at the doorway; he's lying prostrate on the bed. The sun is high in the sky. It should have filled the room but doesn't. She stares out the window. A cloud hovers. Sandra remembers that she's never seen a cloudless sky. Kelvin awaits her response.

"I was just inside fixing something," she quietly tells him. She hopes he doesn't realize that she's lying.

"You are a good woman. I am blessed to have you."

She looks away. But he wants a response and

when he doesn't get one, he stumbles out of the bed. He moves closer to her and pulls her to him. She remains immobile as he presses his body into hers. He kisses her lips and keeps kissing them but her mouth doesn't ease into his. She's only aware of the taste of the rum he's ingested for the past week. His hands touch the curves of her body. She stops him, "Get better first. You're in no state for this."

He nods and returns to bed, where he easily surrenders to its comfort. She hears him snoring. Then she leaves him and picks up the object that he'd stumbled on when he came through the door. She quietly makes her way through the house with it and remembers that while Kelvin sat on the old, hard stool drinking rum, she went with Linden to the seashore. On that day, with the warm sun on their skin, he asked her if she still loves her husband. And she slowly shook her head because she was afraid to mouth the words.

"Marry me," he asked. "I know that we can be happy together because I want to make you paint beautiful canvases. Let's restart our clock."

With the suitcase in tow, she recalls that she looked at him and told him a secret. Two days before Auntie Jeannie died a serious looking man with a suit and briefcase visited her. Behind closed doors, they whispered and a frail Auntie Jeannie called to her after the man left.

"Sandra," her voice was weak and low. "When I

became sick, you took me in and looked after me like I was your own blood. I never had children but you are like my own flesh and blood. Now, I'm going to be a mother to you cause you need one bad bad bad. That man who just left this house is my lawyer. I've left my house with its pretty yard filled with yellow bells to you. And no one else. Nothing goes to your good-for-nothing husband."

Auntie Jeannie saw Sandra's eyes well with gratitude. She gently touched Sandra's hand with her weathered, frail ones. "I can't keep my tongue still anymore. My child, man who love rum, only love rum. He nah go change. Leave my 'wutless' nephew and make a life for yourself."

Sandra looked at the sea then she looked directly at Linden, "Auntie Jeannie gave me more than I ever dreamed or expected. I can paint colours again." Then she rested her head on his shoulder.

Linden was quiet for a long time before he spoke, "I guess you won't take up my offer to run away with me."

"I can't leave my husband for his brother," she slowly responded. "But I still want you in my life. And right now I need your help to move."

"Only if you promise to visit me in Toronto," he added.

She smiles and nods. They sit at the waterside with her head comfortably nestled on his shoulder.

Sandra is now standing at the door. Kelvin's snores are in the background. She takes a final look at the house she's shared with him. Her canvases are no longer on the walls. Linden helped her take them down and hang them at the quaint green house with yellow bells. Her suitcase easily slides out of the doorway. There is no loud thump as she closes the door.

Reading stories was an integral part of my young life while growing up in Antigua. As a child, I wasn't intimidated by the dark, wooden stacks in the library because they excited me. I secretly thought there weren't enough books to fill the library. I was born in 1963, and I spent my childhood in Antigua and Canada. After graduating from Christ the King High School in Antigua, I returned to Canada where I completed a Bachelor of Arts degree from York University. Shortly after completing my degree, I enrolled in a Creative Writing Workshop to explore my desire to write. One workshop led to many others as I discovered my enjoyment of creating stories. After several creative writing classes, memberships in writing groups and through extensive work experience, I developed my writing and editing skills. My first publication was my short story, "Tamarind Stew," in *The Bluelight Corner*, an anthology that featured some of my favourite writers, like Jamaica Kincaid and Alice Walker. In the past, I've hosted a bi-monthly column in the *Guyana Chronicle* that focused on women's issues; and I've also worked as an editor at *Caribarena*. My stories are about the lives of the people in Antigua, the Caribbean, and Toronto, the city where I now reside.

JOANNE C. HILLHOUSE

The Man of Her Dreams

He was a catch. There was no denying that. Violet had worked side by side with him at his campaign office long enough to also know he was a good man; as good a man as one could find in a politician.

He was one of what the now vanquished former leader had called the *nuff and edge up* crowd. Young, impatient for change, educated or uneducated, but, unlike their parents no longer tethered to a party by affection for its long deceased Moses-like founder. They were free to make choices driven by unfamiliar concepts like expectations and performance; young enough to dismiss the compromises that bred political corruption. Perhaps more fatal to the once leader wandering his Hodges Bay home wondering what had happened, they were somehow clued in to something besides the club scene and Facebook. It was the highest voter turnout in Antigua's history. When the dust had settled, Chris Shepherd, a grassroots boy raised by a hardworking Dominican-born grandmother, was the new representative for All Saints West. The man standing next to him, his best man, Warrington

Hughes, had become the first Antiguan leader not to inherit the Prime Minister title like some kind of legacy. It was a hopeful time. They were still 100 days into the new administration, and Chris—whom she'd spent many a late night with as the campaign aide responsible for financing his constituency's campaign— was marrying her best friend Arena. She was happy for Arena: Bright, pretty, never has a bad word to say about anyone, Arena. If she was a little sad for herself, she could ignore that. It would pass.

It had been whirlwind, their romance, like something in the movies. Those who knew Violet might be shocked to discover that she was passionate about romantic comedies. Her favourites were the star-crossed ones, when the magnet of unlikely attraction drew opposites together. *When Harry Met Sally.* "Is one of us supposed to be a dog in this scenario?" *Breakfast at Tiffany's.* "You can always tell the kind of person a man really thinks you are by the type of earrings he gives you." *The Sweetest Mango.* "Nobody's ever given me a mango as a gift before." *Chasing Amy.* "You are the epitome of everything I look for in a human being."

He was, too. Tall. That was important to a woman of her height. Arena was one of those Barbie-sized women who always got the cute, big guys. And he was cute, but not in a too-perfect Billy Dee Williams kind of way (though Billy Dee did have a corner on suave no guy from her generation had quite mastered). Billy Dee and Cary Grant; Chris was almost their love child. Cary's off-kilter charm, Billy's cool, Obama's ears. She liked his Obama ears, like big flapping Dumbo ears, keeping him just this side of too perfect for his own damned good; ears that would have got him enough playground teasing to keep him humble. And he was a humble man; always deferring to her superior knowledge of the numbers, though, masterfully, nudging her towards scraping blood out of stone. "Violet," leaning in close, "If you tell me we can't, we can't. But I'm telling you, we need to. The community needs this. You sure you can't find a little extra five cents under the cushion? I was raised by a woman and I know you all always have money set aside for a rainy day. Stop holding out on me." And he'd have her smiling and blushing, and wanting to move, hell, even Mount Obama for him.

She'd felt herself sinking. Welcomed the fantasies even, felt like it had been forever since anyone had made her feel anything. So much so, she'd started to think that love only existed in movies and that maybe all she was meant for was numbers. "Violet, always with her head in a book," everyone said. And in the 35-and-over danger zone, she'd told herself that that wasn't so bad.

Now, here this boy was (at 30, to her 36, she felt okay calling him "boy" in her mind) stirring things in her. And she was sinking, sinking. Sinking as she watched him light up the crowd at a campaign rally, full of youthful energy and undeniable charisma. Sinking as she watched him doze, mouth hanging open as they drove back from this or that event. Sinking as she watched him kneel down to a child's level to help tie a shoelace. Sinking as old women squeezed his cheeks, and young women blushed and whispered and squealed in his presence. Sinking as he walked her to her door, like they were returning from a date, instead of another long day of "Reclaiming Antigua for the People of Antigua." Sinking as the numbers blurred, and he leaned in close and urged her to make miracles, which she did, for him. Sinking, like the bloody *Titanic*, even after Arena gushed about his expressed interest in her and flashed the ring he'd slipped her but made her promise not to wear until after the election.

She couldn't hate either of them. Not him, for he was, despite setting his sights elsewhere, the man of her dreams. Not Arena, who when all volunteers had shown up that first day, had squeezed in next to her and said, "I'm so excited; I've never done anything like this before…he's cute isn't he?"

Unexpectedly, they'd become friends; Arena, fresh out of college, proving such a capable accounts assistant she'd have no problem writing a letter of recommendation for her once the campaign was done.

Violet already had a job, and worked at the campaign office on her off hours. So, it was extremely fortuitous that Arena, all appearances aside, did have a brain in her head.

She watched them now, saying their vows, in the packed cathedral, and even now, couldn't begrudge them this; even as her heart broke a little.

The reception hall was packed and Violet was glad for the distraction her role as best friend of the bride provided. She ran around lighting a match under the wait staff, making sure everyone's glass was topped up in time for the toast, sipping the remainders, making sure everyone was seated where they should be, glad handing like the politician she wasn't; anything to distract herself from the blinding smile of the couple on the dais. It wasn't going badly really.

She pushed the five layer, rose pink cake into the spotlight just as the father of the bride wound down from his rambling, drunken speech. King Soul, whose "Taking This One" had been the calypso hit of the campaign and who had ably served as platform jester-slash-emcee, was the wedding's emcee. "There she is now to say a few words," he said without missing a beat, "ole money bags herself. Violet, come say something to the people."

She froze.

Violet was a backstage sort of player, and she liked it that way. But the hootin' and hollerin' of the crowd gave no quarter. She took the microphone that Soul held out to her with that big stupid, guileless grin on his face.

"I, uh, thank you, uh, congratulations, uh, to the bride and groom," she said. And would have ended it there, but there was an expectant air in the room, almost as if the crowd could see through her to the yearning she couldn't confess.

She felt hot and cold, and light-headed, and the crowd of maybe 200 friends and family felt like the rally crowd of thousands.

"Uh, I…"

Inexplicably, she felt like crying. This was it, she thought, her moment of possibility gone forever, in public view, and un-mourned. She wasn't a sentimental woman, not usually, her affection for romantic comedies aside, but she felt nostalgic for the life and love she'd never known.

Soul moved as if to take the microphone, just when a voice started speaking, a voice she was shocked to realize was hers.

"I envy the way they look at each other. He looks at her like she's the only woman in the world. Like the day begins and sets there and he has to anchor himself by its rising and setting, its position in the sky. Is it directly overhead? Then that explains this scorching heat, the sweat dripping down my brow. Is she lighting up in glorious colours? Then it must explain the cooling warmth spreading throughout me and the urge to take and kiss, and love, for never was there anything so beautiful. He looks at her like she is everything. Who doesn't want to be looked at like that?"

Soul's hand was frozen midair, and the crowd was silent, not a shuffle or a cough.

Violet cleared her throat.

"When that look is returned with equal fervour, well that is everything, isn't it? If you don't have that what does anything mean? Getting up, going to work, breathing in, breathing out, the slow tedious crawl to death; without someone to look at you, someone for you to look at with such adoration, it's just life isn't it, not really living."

She turned to them then, where they sat, flanked by her father and mother on the one side and the Prime Minister and his grandmother on the other side. His grandmother was elegantly silver-haired, and wore a striking green suit and puzzled smile, canting her head forward as though to hear better.

"Don't ever stop looking at each other like that," Violet said. "The rest of us should be so lucky."

Everything sped up. Soul took the microphone, the crowd applauded, Arena and Chris kissed, and Violet took a tumble like a felled tree, face forward, off the stage. Fade to black.

That night she dreamt she had lost something vital; like her keys or bank card. She spent the entire dream searching under cushions and wandering down streets. She struggled up from sleep, disconcerted. The first thing she spied was her keys on the end table. She had no recollection of getting into bed, her bed. But there she was, fully clothed, and alone, still with that lingering sense of something missing.

She sprinted back to sleep. This time, he was there. But he was turned away from her, and even when she turned him around he hid his face from her. They were Karen and Milton in *From Here to Eternity*, on a beach somewhere, more than enough to choose from in Antigua whose beaches were her pride and joy; the soundtrack swelling around them, and the sun backlit him so she still couldn't see his face. Her lines in his mouth: "I never knew it could be like this. Nobody ever kissed me the way you do."

Violet started, as though waking from a nightmare; this time with a bitter taste in her mouth, that taste lingering even after she'd brushed her teeth. It was late afternoon, of another day by this time, and she'd completely skipped her hangover. Thank God for small blessings.

There was a message on her voice mail from Arena. "We're off, Violet. Thanks for everything. Hope you feel better."

Photo by Emile Hill

If there's anything common to the main characters in Joanne C. Hillhouse's three books—Vere in the *Boy from Willow Bend*, Selena and Michael in *Dancing Nude in the Moonlight*, Nikki in her first full length novel due to be published, at this writing, by Simon and Schuster imprint, Strebor—it's perhaps that they're all people trying to find their place in the world. Issues of loss and identity compel the investigations of the Antiguan writer; as does a commitment to rendering her characters' experiences authentically. Her fiction has, therefore, been described as "honest" and "real," while its flow has been called "poetic" and "lyrical" by various critics. Joanne C. Hillhouse is Antiguan through and through but believes in the power of genuine human experience to transcend cultural barriers. Born in Antigua, her influences were not only homegrown, especially the calypso which she's said provided some of her first lessons in writing, but foreign, from the books she devoured like pepperpot to the TV, films, and songs from faraway places which nonetheless touched something in her. Introspective by nature, it was perhaps inevitable that Joanne would become a writer; and the Ottos native set upon the bumpy, road less travelled. Joanne's dogged persistence has yielded several milestones: the teaching of both *Willow Bend* and *Dancing Nude* in secondary schools in Antigua; an international fellowship to the prestigious Breadloaf Writers' Conference and participation in various other writing programmes and festivals; a UNESCO Honour Award for her contribution to the literary arts and more recently the David Hough Literary Prize from the Caribbean Writer; and publication in numerous Caribbean and international literary journals. Joanne's pride, though, is perhaps the writing programme she initiated in Antigua in 2004, the Wadadli Youth Pen Prize (*http://wadadlipen.wordpress.com*). The aim of the prize is to create the kind of nurturing environment for young writers that was lacking when she was a youth dreaming what she then believed to be an impossible dream. The University of the West Indies grad freelances in her field working on film, internet, TV, radio and print projects. Find her online at *www.jhohadli.com*

CLIFTON JOSEPH

Chuckie Prophesy

'im wuk
innah wan smelly
sweaty
stinkin'
\ dutty FAC'TRY
innah de daytime
nighttime
earlymorningtime
fuh very likkle likkle money
but come de WEEKENDTIME
BACKSIDE: IM FLASHY FLASHY FLASHY
see im poppin style innah im CADILLAC
watch im pull innah de station
fuh some GAS/O/LINE
hear im as he tips im FEATHERED/FEDORA/HAT
ayyyyyy Jack: fill she up...
wid a dollar's worth of GAS/O/LINE
watch im as he digs innah de pockets
of im THREE/PIECE/GAB-ER-DINE
an shift innah im CHICAGO/GANGSTER/LEAN
im cussin like hell

dat MONDAY will come again AGAIN
an interrupt im WEEKEND/PARTY
CONSOLING/PARTLY
DANCING/HAUGHTI-
LY time
in dis here
COLD/COLD/COLD NORTHERN CLIME
TIME WILL COME AROUND
WHEN CHUCKIE'S DISGRUNTLED FROWNS
WILL SEND SKYSCRAPERS/ON/FIRE
TUMBLING
DOWN
DOWN
DOWN
DOWN DOWN DOWN
DOWN DOWN DOWN DOWN
DOWN DOWN DOWN DOWN DOWN
DOWN DOWN DOWN TO THE GROUND
IN   THESE   HERE   NORTHERN
BABYLON/TOWNS.

*footnote to the end of a love affair

…and hey
by the way
what about yesterday?

(as footsteps bounce off concrete
away into the now-barren night
skyscraper-washed white
of all delight)

WHAT ABOUT YESTERDAY?

RITES/FOR WALTER RODNEY

promises heaved in the billowing wind
 are smoke
smiles/grimace/grins
sympathies painted for the occasion-only
only smother the connections of emotions
the winged horse is caught in the spearman's anger
dig the grimace!
See the neck snap
in a final death swing
towards the ashen sky!

Buttressed against a pantheon of myths
the sun burns a spiral into the Ocean
(oh Icarus: why why why the sky?
Why so near the burning sun?)
…and here
the night unfurls its blanket
pouring darkness in profusion
but oh how this night
this occasion
even this old ritual seems new/

seems changed:
Another man has been killed!
Another death/upon/deaths/supersaturated
another man has been killed!
Pull stars from the skies
see the promises already evaporated

In the desert
elephants hurl curled sounds
thru the sandy haze
thru oppression's crafty maze
towards the open sky
BAP//
SHEEBAM//
SHEEBOOM//:
THE SPIRIT SEARCHING FOR CONNECTION
to see the world for what it is
and for what it can be
to tell truths
that show the blue mist rising
that show the sun shining
to make the old, courting despair, laugh
to become the beggarman/chink
in the king's palace/armour
to see the causes
to see the effects
to see the need for action
to be unafraid

of the quiet cold of death
to fall
to rise to be cut down
to rise AGAIN

So merchant-adventurers of the new order
aggress the soul
they kill a man:
hot blood spanning the distance
in the debrised air
broken flesh, strewning a macabre pattern
towards the hot earth
THAT THE WAY
SOMETIMES CANNOT BE BUT BLOOD
IS A RED/DRIPPING/TRUTH
THAT HANGS IN THE LONG NIGHT:
A REFERENT TO OUR DILEMMA:
the dark quiet room
the demerara cage
the bird's blooded broken wings
they try to stifle the spirit
they can not
they will try
but the spirit pulls
as the equinoxes pull
and plants the seeds
in the souls of the dead
and in the wombs of the unborn

THE NIGHT IS LONG
AND THE MORNING'S LIGHT
DOES NOT SHINE
UNLESS YOU FIGHT
FIGHT
FIGHT
FIGHT
FOR IT

Dubzz/poet/at/large Clifton Joseph is a poet and journalist who has written for television, radio, newspapers, and magazines.

A founding member of the dub poetry movement in Canada, he has published a book of poems, *Metropolitan Blues*; *Oral/Trans/Missions*, an album of poetry and music; the videos "Pimps" and "(Survival) In the City," as well as numerous single dub poetry releases including "A Chant For Monk," "That Night In Tunisia," and "Shots On Eglinton."

He has performed widely across Canada, the US, the UK, and the Caribbean and his poems have been included in a number of written and audio anthologies including "Poetry Nation" and "Word Up," a Virgin Records compilation of North American performance poets.

Among Joseph's awards are two Gemini Awards for Best Writing in an Information Program or Series; a Time-Warner "Freddies" Award for excellence in health reporting; a Silver Fleece Award from the Chicago International Film Festival; and the Best Dub Poet Award and the Peter Tosh Memorial Award from the Canadian Reggae Music Awards.

Joseph was born in New Winthropes Village, Antigua and Barbuda, and now lives in Toronto, Canada.

DWAYNE MORGAN

Tight-Lipped

It would seem to me,
that the only genre
where we are overrepresented on the TV,
would be the evening news,
and I'm getting tired of watching women crying,
pleading for witnesses and clues,
which we know will never come,
because we stay tight-lipped,
protecting the guilty,
while innocence is washed away
like blood from crime scenes.
We,
were once a courageous people,
but look at how far we've fallen;
we attend more funerals
than weddings;
we've become society's joke,
honouring the code of the street,
more than we respect the life of the deceased.
It could so easily be
your mother, your sister, or your brother
on that TV screen,

and when it is,
who do you expect to care?
It seems clear
that we are happier in police stats,
and starring on newscasts
than taking our community back.
We stay tight-lipped,
giving more power to those killing us,
than those uplifting us;
backwards mindset,
so we never come forward.
We used to die for a cause,
now we die just because,
and I wonder how this could be.
In which direction should my finger point its blame
when the victim and suspect both look like me?
As a right of passage,
maybe every black boy,
starting at the age of ten,
will pose for a formal picture on his birthday,
to be used on the news when he is gunned down;
that might be the closest we ever get
to offering dignity to our dead,
and I can't help but feel confused.
As a community,
we remain tight-lipped,
about what's going on,
when we're the only ones
getting screwed.

The Ethnic Vote

The census confirms that I exist,
Yet I am the invisible Canadian,
Whose experiences and concerns are ignored,
Except for when an election is called.
Suddenly, everyone cares about the plight
Of those who identify as non-white;
They call me the ethnic vote.
Our votes are like lottery numbers,
The more of them you have,
The better your chances at winning,
So we hold candidates hostage
With our ballots,
Watching as the roles reverse
And we are now the ones in power.
There can be no majority,
Without us minorities,
So we wait to see who will have the courage
To put their promises in writing,
Because talk is cheap,
And our experiences are too rich
To be given away with nothing in return,

So photo ops with souvlaki and butter chicken
Won't be enough this time around.
Mrs. Singh and Mr. Chow,
Are now demanding more,
And this is the new face of Canada,
A new reality that must be addressed
If we are to move forward.
Multiculturalism has to be more than rhetoric,
Because we are more than just a strategy
To get you into office,
More than a statistic,
More than just a demographic to be conquered,
Like many of our homelands.
Who will show us that they care and truly understand?
We are a land suffering from a shortage of medical staff,
yet we have policies that keep doctors driving taxicabs.
Who will speak for the faces
Being displaced to gentrification?
We are a nation that still fears what lies behind the veil,
As we tighten our borders to keep the undesirables out.
We still don't recognize
That when the funding of our youth is cut,
The growth of our most needy and brilliant is also cut.
When having young people play on monkey bars
Is less important than having them play behind bars,
There needs to be a shift in our thinking.
We are still a country that has Native women disappearing
Faster than their land, rights, and autonomy,

What promises can you make to me

That you can actually keep?

Up until now,

You've been see-through like windows,

And we've seen enough.

We are sick of promises,

And are demanding actions.

Who will speak to us in our language

With empathy and compassion,

Knowing that our experience of being Canadian,

Is just as diverse as our cultures?

We are the new face of this country,

And without us,

The future lacks hope.

So we'll be saving our decisions until election day.

Sincerely,

The Ethnic Vote.

Hoop Dreams

Black boy with hoop dreams,
Wants to be the greatest like Mike;
He never goes out
Without a fresh pair of Jordans.
Scouts at every game
Claim him as the king of the city.
He has his eyes on the prize,
But his focus on breasts and thighs
Often gets in the way.
School wasn't an investment worth his time,
But a necessary evil.
He lacked the dedication of a Maverick.
No matter how many classes he missed,
He always got a free pass,
Because he was the key to the championship.
The NBA wasn't just a dream,
But a guarantee,
With his skills,
And the numbers on his stat sheets.
He couldn't shake his weakness for the women
Who'd swarm him like Hornets;

Young ones that were easy to lay up;
Older ones with their biological shot clocks ticking.
His attitude was Cavalier like a Chevy,
But he knew when to turn up the Heat.
He was a Wizard,
Travelling from hood to hood,
Making women dribble with the thought
That they might be the one
He chooses to spend
Three seconds in their key,
Before fouling out the door of their love Shaq.
He was a Warrior,
Not concerned with Knicks and Spurs,
He'd work them like Pistons,
Often forgetting to put a shooting guard on his small forward,
Before putting his hardwood in her centre,
With the intensity of Rockets,
Rolling through Thunder,
As he'd shoot his dreams like Bullets,
Into every basket on the playground.
He was living it up,
But the crossover came,
When women started showing up at each game,
Sitting on the bench,
With buns in their stomachs,
Rising like the Phoenix Sun.
He tried to ignore it,
But there was no Magic fix.

Each woman would sit,
Wearing her embarrassment,
Realizing that she'd been flagrantly fouled,
And wasn't the only one.
His issues outside of the gym,
Had his stock dropping
Like three-point shots.
Things were unravelling like old jerseys.
He was spending more time in the court
Than on the court,
Trying to block all of the charges,
Crying Doc Rivers
No longer on the team;
He went from a guarantee
Of the good life,
To multiple mouths to feed.
Reality was a slam dunk,
Being replayed each night,
Leaving him with nothing, but a hoop dream.

Name Calling

They called us Niggers;
Considered us less than human,
Chattel, that could be bought and sold.
They called us Niggers,
A people displaced,
Original names erased,
Replaced by the unfamiliar.
They called us Niggers,
As they branded names and numbers
Into our skin;
Niggers as they stripped us of our dignity,
Niggers as they whipped us into submission,
Niggers as they raped our women,
Niggers at Sunday afternoon family lynchings,
Yet we say, what's in a name?
We call them our enemies;
People on the other side of the world
Whom we've never met.
We call them terrorists,
As we prepare to attack their sovereignty.
We call them insurgents,

Subjects to be eliminated,
Before bombing them off of the earth.
We call them threats to our democracy
And way of life,
Before destroying their land,
Agreeing to build it back,
With McDonald's and Starbucks
Americanizing the world's palate,
One conflict at a time.
Yet we say, what's in a name?
There is a switch in the human brain,
A part of our psyche and spirit,
That for the majority of us,
Is set to good,
Stifling our desires to do others harm,
But there's power in names;
We use them to dehumanize
And justify our actions;
It's the only way to get past that place
Of goodness within us.
We use words to turn good people into killers,
The naïve into slaveholders,
Men into abusers;
It starts in the parks and playgrounds,
As bullies assert their will;
It continues in school hallways,
As self-esteem is destroyed.
These names are loaded like handguns,

Ready to do damage to their targets.
We call them bitches
Before hitting them with our fists,
Bitches as we extract sexual pleasure
With no care for their person,
But what's in a name?
We call ourselves Niggers,
Not brothers, kin, or men,
Because we see ourselves as less than human.
We call ourselves Niggers
As we brandish guns,
Ready to take the life of a woman's son,
Because it's easy to kill anything that's beneath us,
Anything that we deem less than,
Or give no worth at all.
Every day we choose to build or destroy,
Depending on the names that we call.

Man Up

There is no manual for manhood,
No manuscript,
With carefully crafted characters
And scripts to be manipulated
By mankind.
Consider this, my Manifesto,
For men from Mandeville to Manchester,
Mannheim to Manhattan,
Who are told to man up
When faced with human emotions.
This is for the lost boys,
Frozen like mannequins,
In the bodies of men,
Who suffer in silence,
Innocence manhandled,
Abused at church or hockey practice,
Unable to let go of things that aren't their fault.
Man up!
Stop being so soft!
This is for those mangled spirits,
Seeking the freedom to be vulnerable,

Fearing failure,
Managing the shame of defeat in private;
Man up!
Never let them see you break!
This is for those men,
Who aren't men,
Because they love men;
On a manhunt for acceptance,
And their masculinity,
Going manic,
Trying to fit into his,
And this, box.
Sissy, Man up!
This is for those manufactured real men,
With tear ducts sealed like manhole covers,
Because real men don't cry,
And I am constantly questioning myself,
Wondering about my own identity,
Because tears manifest within,
And flow out of me regularly.
I am not one who believes
That it is mandatory for men to be hard,
Devoid of emotion.
Look at the world that men have built;
We've got to become more female,
If we ever hope to truly be human.
Manhood is as individual as raindrops,
And who can stop the rain from falling?

Put old notions on the mantle,

Because even a softy like me

Feels manly when holding my daughter to my chest

While she sleeps,

Playing princesses, dress up,

And having tea parties.

Who gets to decide if a guy like me,

Is man enough to be a man?

Whose standard are we using?

What's the criteria and mandate?

Dude, are you gay?

Man up!

Forget that chick!

Man up!

Your back really hurts that bad?

Man up!

Why are you being so soft?

Man up!

That was years ago! Let it go!

Man up!

Why do you even care?

Man up!

When everything that makes us human,

Is followed by man up,

I wonder if there'll ever be a time,

When I can be man enough.

We Are the Ones

To be a gift,
Born into this world male,
Packaged in black wrapping paper,
Is to be constantly reminded
That you are disposable,
That your life lacks meaning and value,
And isn't protected by the law.
There is no pretty bow
Or designs on your packaging;
You live knowing that justice is a drunk
Who will not be served.
We, the black gifts,
are the first to be accused
And the last to be believed.
We are the guilty until proven innocent,
The aggressor despite the evidence.
We are the hoops
For which loopholes are made;
The ones who fight daily
For their dignity.
We are the Sambos,

The puppets,
Our worth based on the value
We bring our puppeteers,
So dance negro dance,
Rap black boy rap,
Run nigga run,
But what about those of us
Who are regular,
Who are average,
Who don't have special talents
That society wants or loves,
We are just their packaging,
Bodies wrapped in black skin,
Stuck on modern day plantations
being abused at will,
And people wonder why we seldom smile,
And why it seems like our looks could kill.
We are the ones who put basketballs
In our sons' palms
Before they can talk,
And only dribble,
With the hope that they will grow
To dribble beyond their packaging.
We are the ones who make elevators go quiet,
Purses and loved ones clenched tighter.
We are the deer that stare
at the barrel of guns,
But there is no licence needed to hunt us.

I am the suspicious package
At the airport,
Or in any store with goods
That we aren't supposed to be able to afford,
Whether I'm in a hoodie or a suit;
Accused of driving while black
In minivans or coupes.
We are the black licorice
discarded at Halloween,
The silhouette
used for target practice by the police.
We are the black men
Who want nothing more
Than to be human,
With respect and dignity;
So this is for every Trayvon, Jaekwon,
Marcus, Jordan, Dwayne,
Every gift wrapped in black skin,
Considered a nigger
Despite having a name.
This is for everyone
who feels the pain of race,
for the empty seat
Beside a black man on the train.
We are the ones who cry constantly
When we see,
People being killed for no reason
Who look just like me.

We are the ones who meet death
On cold asphalt,
Discarded like roadkill.
We are the ones;
Worthless gifts,
Packaged in black wrapping paper
That nobody wants.
We are the voiceless.
We are the ones.

Dwayne Morgan began his career as a spoken word artist in 1993. In 1994, while still in high school, he founded Up From The Roots entertainment, to promote the positive artistic contributions of African Canadian and urban influenced artists.

A member of the Writers' Union of Canada, Morgan has received both the African Canadian Achievement Award, and the Harry Jerome Award for Excellence in the Arts. Morgan is the winner of three Canadian Urban Music Awards (2001, 2003, 2005). In 1998, Morgan introduced regular poetry slams to

Toronto, and has watched them blossom across the GTA and beyond ever since. In 2005 he was recognized as Poet of Honour at the Canadian Festival of Spoken Word in Vancouver. In 2008 Morgan's contribution to the Arts and Canadian society were recognized on the Legacy Black History Month poster.

Dwayne has published six books, most recently, *Her Favourite Shoes* (2011), which followed, *The Sensual Musings of Dwayne Morgan* (2010), *The Making of A Man* (2005), *The Man Behind The Mic* (2002), *Long Overdue* (1999), and chapbooks, *The Revolution Starts Within* (1996), and *Straight From The Roots* (1995). In 2009, Morgan's work was translated into French, culminating in the book, *Le Making of d'un Homme*. He has also released six albums. His albums include, *Another Level* (1997), *The Evolution* (2001), *Soul Searching* (2003), *A Decade in the Making* (2004), *Mellow Mood: The End of the Beginning* (2007), and *Idle Hands* (2011). In 2008, Morgan released a commemorative DVD entitled, *Dwayne Morgan The First Fifteen*.

Dwayne has performed for the former Governor General of Canada, The Honourable Michaëlle Jean, and has shared the stage with many of Canada's top artists including Russell Peters, Deborah Cox, Kardinal Offishal, Jully Black, K-OS, and Nelly Furtado, while opening for international artists Alicia Keys, Linton Kwesi Johnson, Mutabaruka, Ursula Rucker, Colin Channer, and Saul Williams, and recording with

Canadian artists including Grammy nominee, Drake.

To further explore his creativity, Dwayne collaborated with Driftwood Studios to film, *Three Knocks*, a ten-minute film based on his domestic violence poem of the same name, which premiered in Toronto's Reel World Film Festival. In March 2008, Dwayne hosted his first photography exhibit, *The Sum of Her Parts*, exploring female body image.

MOTION

Locks and Love

The baby is crushed against my chest. I know I should have worn my long coat, but honestly, it's not as cute. And besides, I had to have the inside pocket, so I could hide a cassette—a mixtape I made, all the tunes. I know I could have waited in McDonald's, but then I might end up at the back of the line. Last time I did that, I got crushed up in the front between two old ladies and their picnic baskets. Not me today. I'll just soldier it out.

My eyes are still burning, and I don't talk to anyone when we get on. I guess that's what I get for staying up all night. I'm too nervous to sleep. I keep dreaming about running and missing the ride. I'd try to yell, but the words would just fall to my feet. So, I sat up, redid the front of my braids, packed up the diaper bag, made the tape, and watched my son sleep as the sky lightened behind the highway and the Christmas lights.

———————————————

The van is jammed by the time we hit Scarborough pick up. Sometimes, you'd think people would stay home, but no. Come good or bad weather, they are here. Today, I have to hold the baby and the diaper bag on my lap. I just close my eyes, because then I can go back to that party. We're just beating juice, the DJ drops this wicked old school lovers rock. I feel something behind me. The body eases up close. When his arms come around my waist, I can smell sunshine above the weed smoke. He bends into me, his face close to my neck. *A million times or more I thought about you.* That was before the arrest, before the baby, before the trial. Before is a long time ago.

I still look for him in the street. Sometimes, I'm about to turn the corner to my door, and I imagine he's standing there, waiting for us. We go inside. He takes care of the baby while I cook up some ital food. But then the corner turns, and the hallway is empty. Just music blasting out of somebody's crib. I twist my key, and shut the door on the mirage.

When I was little, I used to have an imaginary boyfriend. He'd push me on the swing in the schoolyard, or sometimes we'd walk home and hold hands. I'd be sitting on the couch watching TV, and his arm would come around me. And at night, when we'd lay under the covers, his lips would sweep mine like the wind. I was never alone.

I feel a tap on my back. For the past twenty minutes, this child's been bawling down the place. He's trying to walk these days, so now he's not trying to sit in one place. He fought off the bottle, the rattle, the back rub, the jiggle, the up and down on the knee. He's so loud. You can't even hear the static on the radio.

I feel the finger dig on my back again. *Pass that boy over here.* I feel my palms open and release him into hands stretching over my shoulder. I turn and watch him as he's passed back like a relay, over the rows of seats. He lands in a lap that sits by the corner. She doesn't even look at me. But she makes a face, and he laughs. I fall back in my seat and watch in the rear-view as she turns him to face the window. The van is quiet again, and the static plays on.

When I was younger, I used to roll with this girl called Marcia. All of us used to hang, chilling on the steps at school, chatting people and causing ruction. One time, she invited us to sleepover. When we reached, it was just her and her moms, living in this cute apartment. Just them. No man throwing shit around, making up noise. No brothers, no sisters crowding you up. Just them, living all the way down there in some place called Esplanade. Back then I thought to myself, one day, that's how I'm gonna live, quiet and peaceful, just me and my youth....

Lemme get a condom, he told me.
But you said forever, right?

My hearts pounds when I jump out my sleep. The van is veering off the highway, and there's no baby on my chest. I spin around, but the lady who held him before has her face pasted up against the window with some knitting under her chin. I feel an elbow dig me in my side, the lady beside me pouts her lips up towards the front. I see over the hills of shoulders, he's wrapped up in a next woman's arms.

The ark opens when we get into Kingston. I almost know all the stops now. Millbrook, then K.C., Collinswood, and after that Gravenhurst. I watch a woman drag her cooler out from under the seats, a man wearing that green winter jacket, pacing by the front steps. When the door slams, they fall into a hug. He grabs the cooler in one hand and her waist in the other. The van busts a U-turn, and we head towards the stone walls.

"Mommy, look. Daddy's castle." A little kid voice fills up the van. I press my baby into my ribs. He watches and the roof appears like hot clay against the sky. The driver says he'll be back in two hours. Then he pulls off, and we're left in front of the door, the bars and wire. A guard drives past us, eyeing over the top of his shades. We wait for the buzzer, a voice to crack over the intercom, the click of the door. Two hands heave it open.

At the Don, you only had to sign in. But then, you had to wait in that line, stand up against the counter, talk on a phone through the thick glass. Here it's *What's your name, Who are you here to see, Sign the next line, Lock up your belongings*. Then they want your ID, your earrings, your necklace. They wipe them with their cloth and put it through their scan. She empties my baby bag, jiggles the jar food, shakes the sleeper and the blanket. Holds the rattle to the light. She waits for the machine to beep. I don't. I grab up my things, and cross the border.

Black liquid squirts steam into a Styrofoam cup. A few card games going on, kids running on the mat, somebody's trying not to argue in the corner. At the table beside me, a woman caresses the leaves of her Bible. The gold edges strobe like the fluorescents on the ceiling. I turn every time the door clicks.

He's fresh shaved when he comes in; his hair in a big 'fro. He crushes us to his chest. I can smell the Kush I slipped in his pocket last time. I can feel he's lost weight. But after a year, the stiffness of his shirt, the boniness of his back feels good. We pass the baby between us, like we do this every day. I don't remember that he never got a chance to rub my belly.

He holds the baby while I part roads into his scalp. I twist my body in the bolted chair, scratch at the dry parts, smooth oil into them. I whisper close to his ear what I'm wearing under my jeans and pick the blue blanket fuzz from the ends of his braids. He says maybe year after next, he can apply for trailer, and we can come spend the whole weekend together, like a family.

I don't bother to tell him about how the baby was sick. I don't tell him the phone almost got cut last week, again. The lie rolls from my mouth when he asks if I've talked to so-and-so lately.

_____

A black Santa. Some of the kids look suspicious, but they run towards him anyway. Fathers peel the plastic from tiny candy canes.

He asks me again, *why doesn't the baby have my last name.* I explain again, *you weren't there to sign the papers.* He insists, again, *something could have been arranged.* I dig the comb into his scalp. I bite my lip, smooth grease between the rows.

_____

The hands on the wall are speeding closer to time. Someone starts to shuffle, gathering up the scraps of their visit, tucking children into coats and pop cans in trash bins. He starts, *when I come out*…I don't catch the rest. I look around the room. I think I hear fifty other sentences starting the same way.

_____

The photo dude stops by to take a picture. Around us, arms squeeze, lips brush, a girl won't let go of her father's leg. We stand by the shiny green tree. I slide the cassette into his pocket.

We always used to kiss with our eyes open. Here, we close our eyes when we say goodbye. I run my palm over his cornrows, his finger slips under the back of my shirt. He puts his face in the baby's neck and inhales. He never lingers, like some of the others do. His back gets straight, he turns, and nods to the guard. He disappears behind the clicking door. I try not to look back but I always do.

———————————

The door claps behind me. I ease into a row as the driver pulls off. Silence, eyes on windows, the day is already dim. The radio pops over the hum of the air vents as the van drones along in the dusk. Heads nod, some stare into the coming darkness. The static clears as we get closer to home.

Graf

You can't catch it
just snatches in frames that
fly past windows
inscripted in insidious
crevices and corners
scrawled on concrete slabs
of underpass

hush
eyes peeled to feel the pressure
of fingers pressed on spray can tips
aerated shades grow bold in phases
stage impromptu shows at the
sides of the road

Burns lay in wait on lost walls
for the next eyes tomorrow
which too will wonder why
these spaces found significance in the
eyes of midnite writers
scribes who
spray legacies of hieros
on the edge of cityscapes

   they'll outlast our past
when our last breath escapes
for these dwellers create
carved calligraphies
and scripts on bricks
tattooed tags stain train's skin
impromptu impressions
impressive dimension
destination, eternal
so lost walls become
heaven

SheLand*

she is the black the blues the golds the red
the sun bursting through the horizon
the victory
the blood

she is the Akan
the face of Asante
Yoruba
the Coromantee

she is woman
grandmother
aunt
daughter
child
she is the coming together
the passing down
the moving on

she is storyteller
keeper of she-story
griot
the rememberer of names

she crossed seas in grave ships
she is the song of memory
the call to resistance

she is the long strain of sugar cane
the tears at its roots
she survives
the sun and wind
as stone mills stand watch from distant hills

she is the commemoration
the emancipation
she is celebrated
she is the town crier to screams freedom from scrolls

she is the benna and calypso
the bang of iron band
she is the brangalang of steel pan
the explosion of the road march
the movement of mas
she is timeless
as j'ouvert morning
the (echo) last lap before it all begins
again
she is the noise of town
the leaning streets
the colonies' last towers
the stone cathedral
the women and baskets
the grand display of wares

she is the stiff turn of cornmeal
the spike of pepper
the fragrance of thyme
the deep heat of ginger beer
and sorrell's red tang

she is Antigua Black
the quench of juice behind her patterned beauty
she is the catching of water
beads of liquid inching down graceful necks
weighted pots balanced on queenly heads

she strolls on moonlight night
curves of road into far-reaching parishes
she is the life blood of the village
the moans of church organs
connecting of homes

she is the constant wave on her border of beaches
she is the replacing of pink sand
the beauty of coral washed to shore

she is fingers caressing seeds on the warri board
she is the sharp crack of cricket bat
running feet
beating hearts
the collective roar

she is hibiscus and bougainvillea
she stands tall as coconut trees
she transplants on jumbo planes
and shines amongst the maple
the pine, the oak leaves

she is young feet on concrete
the crush of filled streets
she floats between the skyscrapers
her brown reflection in the glass
she redefines
she intertwines
she remixes cultures
she becomes

she is 10 x 12 miles x watery stretch x world x universe
she is island she is urban
she knows no borders
her reach spans the globe

she is the unappeased and the unrest
she is the building of nations
she is independence
flags raised and waving
she is representation
she is city
she is bridge
she is nest

she is home
the surviving of lineage
the keeping of kin
the echoes of the Waladli
and footprints Wa'omoni

she swings in the new pleats of uniforms
books clutched in new arms
shoes dusty in island sand
she stands
with good morning prayers
the peal of young voices
unison and national song

she is sneakered feet
and stand on guard for thee
she is the new generation
the hyphenated young

she is the current
the calm and rough of seas
she is the dark in the mist
the trilogy of lands

she is endurance
the sun ups and sun downs
she is the browning of skin
the deep bake of melanin

she is Rocky Cliff and Bogey Peak
she is divine sculptor
she is the wind's hand
the chiselling ocean

she is creation of music
the scribing of poem
the ancient drawings undisturbed
in hidden caves

she is the endeavouring and achieving
the hope and the believing
she is the future
the striving
the laying of legacy

she is the song of memory
the whispering dance
the giant laughter
the quiet dawn
the setting sun
the cricket's night song
the cry that breaks thru the silence of morn
the new day begun

Be Girl

She use to write wet kisses in her rhyme book
use to lead the ritual of the crush, sprinkle, roll
she was b-girl
born to do this
thing that thoughtless folks told her not to do
there's no place for you
under booming systems and block heavy boxes
two inch nails can't grow when u carrying crates
weighted down with wax records
rolling with the man dem through the back doors of
jams
they thought it was *cute*
when young girls caught their groove on
covered down in t-shirts and baggy shorts
battle ready and rebellious
fingers rifle ready
to clack clack   reload!
yeah   she'd beat down
walls as DJs sound clashed in concert hall
she'd kill a soundbwoy
dissect with dialect

gyal waan test just
seckel and rest
seen
   seeds came through her
babies were born
b-girl laid down her arms
and b-woman was born

Motion is a prolific urban artist, manipulating words to their exponential power. Her revolutions around words have generated for audiences a melodic flow that runs deep in its proverbial roots.

Possessing charismatic agility in rap, songwriting, and poetry, this award-winning artist is a keen composer, and intense performer. Motion's career accolades began when she became the first female Hip Hop artist to be nominated for MuchMusic's Best Rap Video. Her pioneering presence continued into the millennium when her commentary on urban life and love in Toronto made her the winner of the CBC National Poetry Face-Off with her nationally acclaimed poem, "Connect the T.Dots."

Motion is the first Hip Hop artist in Canada to publish a collection of writings, *Motion In Poetry* (Women's Press, 2006) with the companion album, the *Audio Xperience*. In the US, the Canadian-born MC represented the northern creative mass when she rocked the Nuyorican Poet's Café, Jimmy's Uptown Poetry Spot in Harlem, Brooklyn's Nkiru Bookstore, the Zulu Nation Anniversary Celebrations, and Russell Simmon's Def Poetry Jam on HBO. This all led to the much-anticipated launch of Motion's latest volume of poetry, *40 Dayz* (Women's Press, 2009).

A recent member of Obsidian Theatre's Playwrights Unit, Motion's latest projects explore characters infused with her natural forte for rhythm and poetical voice. Her plays, *Aneemah's Spot/The Base* and *4our Woman* have been featured at renowned dramatic venues such as The International Black Playwrights Festival, Cross Currents Festival, and the Rock.Paper.Sistaz Festival. Her latest aural/poetical solo work debuted at Toronto's Factory Theatre. Expanding from stage to screen, Motion's screenplay, *Soundgirl*, is now in development with Conquering Lion Pictures. Her newest work-in-progress, co-created with noted director Mumbi and choreographer Meryem, is *Dancing to a White Boy Song*, debuting at the Summerworks Theatre Festival in 2011.

Motion is a regal artist who carries a potent mix of skills, creation, and culture. Noted by *Urbanology Magazine* as "a prolific performer," her ability to capture the cadence and melody of words propels her to consistently produce progressive content. She has become a northern source of organic urban energy, and penetrating poetic persuasion. It's the inherent power in Motion that generates such an illuminating presence.

It's all about expression, and bringing that passion into everything I do. I love music, I love words. So you can hear me, you can read me, you can see me...feel me?
—Motion

JELANI NIAS

Bottles' Hustle

School done. I spent a whole day doing nothing after my graduation. Granny was up and acting like her usual self. She chased me out of the kitchen area with her wooden spoon when I came to boil bush tea and went on to make fritters with some overripe bananas that her "friend" left for us. I ran out of the house with a full belly and a reel of fishing line, hoping to catch flies or a lizard, even a worm, *something* to put on the end of my line since I didn't have the money to buy a small pack of squid. At day's end I skipped home with only a ravenous hunger and a feeling of serenity to show for my adventure and that was all right. Too bad it couldn't last.

Granny P was up before me. Around five o'clock I heard her rustling around in one of the clear plastic bags she stores everything in. I opened my right eye first and glanced around before joining it with the left. Granny was on her bed, a mug of something that was probably tea with a touch of rum on the dresser beside her. In her lap was one of the larger sacks, midway between shopping bag and garbage-bag size, stuffed with a mix of documents, letters, photocopies, and other paper products.

"You wake up," my grandmother noted.

"Morning," I mumbled.

She gave me the side-eyed, measured look that sometimes preceded a lecture but settled for a "hmph" instead. I didn't wait for her to organize her thoughts; I hustled out of the house with my washcloth, soap, toothpaste, and a plastic jug filled with water. Granny is my best friend in some ways, but it's not every day that I can take one of her speeches on posture, ungodly music, my supposed bull-headedness, and the evils of the opposition party. Thankfully, by the time I returned she was engrossed by some document that she'd unfolded from her bag.

"You going out so today?" She asked as I walked in, without looking up from her papers.

"Yes, Granny."

"Don't leave before you eat," she ordered.

"Okay." I put on a pair of jean shorts and looked for a shirt.

"You could go by Mrs. Samuels," Granny P suggested. Mrs. Samuels was a widow with a big house and a huge yard. I instantly put paying her a visit near the top of my agenda; if my grandmother was advising me to pass that way it meant she had probably spoken to the old lady somehow. Lawn work: definitely a good start.

I ate day-old bakes with butter and drank a mug of fever grass tea while Spiderman repaired a web directly over my head. While I chewed I calculated. It was July 10. I had $253 tucked away. I needed to have $3,250 more by August 15 to get into the only high school I viewed as worth attending. It seemed then, sitting there in the chair next to the stove that my life was like some fumbled object dancing off my fingertips, somewhere between floating and a fatal crash. This summer was my split-second chance to grab it firmly.

By 7:30 am I was walking Nova Madeira's main strip with an empty garbage bag. The sun was out and bright. I imagined that the rays were really the glare of search lamps mounted atop the invisible walls of the prison I was escaping. Shadows were the only safe places. I slunk around the area, trying to stay shaded, darting out only when there was treasure worth risking the light for. Our little village has never had a real commercial district, but the Strip with its KFC, its pharmacy, its bars, and the pizza shop is usually urban enough for me to find about a half-dozen recyclable bottles. (As far as that went, the real haul would come when I got to town, but every fifty cents added up.) The bottles I pretended were keys. I decided that if I could find six I'd have enough to break free. I found seven and made my way towards Mrs. Samuels' home feeling blessed by the good omen.

The first hint that my day was not to be as idyllic

as the seven bottles had suggested came within shouting distance of the widow's place. I was walking purposefully in loose dirt next to a hot stretch of paved road, my game of sunshine-pretend having long since withered under the dry heat. My mostly empty bag of recyclables swung with each step, the multi-layered smacking sounds helping to keep my spirits high as they clinked (*three dollars*) and clanked (*and fifty cents*). I was a few steps short of the final turn along the roadside when the mobile weight of a speeding truck came ripping towards me, its hurtling mass leaning in the direction of the corner, all giant wheels, yellow paint, and chrome bumper. Two of its four wheels had strayed across the line between road and soil. Dry fountains of earth sprayed behind and to the side of what was, to me, a monstrous mechanical assembly of potential murder. Within moments it was gone, reduced to nothing more than a dwindling noise and some lingering, black smoke, but not before whipping dirt against my shins and passing close enough for the breeze left in its wake to tussle my camouflage shirt. Had I but reached out a hand to touch it, I would've probably been left with an arm that ended in a stump just above the elbow.

"Fuck!" I yelled, trembling with adrenalin, spent fear and limp anger. Whoever was driving that thing could easily have killed me, actually came very close to doing so, and up to now he hadn't even slowed down.

The idea that perhaps he hadn't seen me never crossed my young, self-important mind. I felt personally aggrieved; this was a part of the loose but pervasive conspiracy against my person that was the devil's hallmark. Following Granny's advice I said a quick "get behind me Satan" and let it go. A moment or two and I set off again.

Less than five minutes later I was striding towards Mrs. Samuels' yard with dust in my shoes but none the worse for wear. I got nervous when I saw that her sprawling lawn was freshly cut, hedges neatly trimmed. Had someone stolen the food from my plate while I was corralling beer bottles and dodging sun rays? With rapidly descending expectations I approached the widow's front door and gave it three respectful knocks.

"Who is it?" Mrs. Samuels sang-called from inside.

"Good morning, Mrs. Samuels. It's Bottles. I just checking if you have anything you need done today."

The door opened, revealing the older woman's short, wide frame. Mrs. Samuels was one of those sixty-plus women who seem ornery enough to wrestle a young man and strong enough to win. She stood there on heavy legs, arms with wrists as big as my ankles folded over massive breasts that I always struggled not to look at, and a look of mild regret on her dark face.

"But why you come so late? Since weekend I here hoping you would pass by and can't see you. It's just yesterday I finally get tired a watching this big, bushy yard turn jungle and give somebody else the work." I must have really looked crestfallen because the woman promised me a job washing her windows at the end of the week. I smiled my brightest, most fake smile and thanked her for her consideration. Then I was back on the road.

The fifth car waved at offered to take me to a turn on New Castle Road that was maybe a half mile outside of Sevilla Heights, which itself was a suburb of my final destination, St. Paul. It was a nice car, a Honda of some sort, clean both inside and out and driven by a pretty, stylish woman in her mid-forties who looked like someone that dirt wouldn't have the audacity to settle on.

"So, young man," she said as I climbed into her air-conditioned environs and closed the door behind me, "tell me your name." On the radio Whitney Houston was putting her last vocal impressions on "The Greatest Love of All."

"My name is Devon, but people here call me Bottles," I explained.

"Devon is a very nice name. It *suits* you. You look like a Devon, yes. Pleased to meet you, I'm Patricia."

I knew she was cool with those two words: "I'm Patricia." Most adults would have said Mrs. or Mr. So-and-so, emphasizing the caste differences between those who had already achieved the age of majority and me as a juvenile. That she hadn't looked good on her.

Patricia turned up the radio as a male announcer began to give headlines for the upcoming news report. I looked out the window and let my mind wander as blankly as possible, watching with detachment as my village of Nova Madeira gave way and then fell behind me.

"Time for a change, yes! Full time we snatch the purse strings back from these crooks," my new friend said suddenly, snatching my attention back from the road.

I tried to catch what it was on the radio that had prompted such an excited response, but the first strains of "Ramajay" from Machel Montano were obliterating whatever political blurb had riled up my benefactor. She laughed when she caught me looking. "Sorry Devon, I'm sure you don't care about no old woman's politics, but it's a real promising time for our country and it will affect you too. It look like we might finally get rid of these UWP...." Patricia stopped short of calling our national, ruling party a name and laughed instead.

Somehow, the subject moved to basketball and stayed there for the rest of the ride. Pat, as she soon instructed me to call her, was knowledgeable about the game and both of us were Cleveland fans. The ride seemed all too short. Watching her car accelerate off a while later, I wondered how such a smart-seeming woman could so dislike the United Wadumein

Party. Maybe she didn't know about the Scholastic Achievers' Program, or their plan to introduce universal secondary education.

The walk to Sevilla Heights seemed longer than it was. I stalked along the road like a panther with padded footfalls, imagined myself attacking the cars that whooshed past. Creeping beside homes with old, fruit laden trees and dogs in the yard, I became an animal tamer coaxing snarling, barking dogs into uneasy truces. It was not until I entered the first yard, the Da Souzas', that I became Bottles again. And I was definitely Bottles, not Devon; Devon was for home, school, and church. Bottles was a working name.

A chorus of deep-throated canine aggression greeted my first steps towards the electric powered iron gate. I ignored them, knowing that as long as I was on this side of the grill they had no way of reaching me. This was where the great man lived, the minister of education himself, the author of the Scholastic Achievers' Program that would soon be sending me through the portals of academia to places around the world. I met him once. He shook my hand, asked me what school I went to and then surprised me by knowing my principal by name. But it wasn't him I was there to see. He might be responsible for the education portfolio in Wadumein, but it was his maid, Mrs. Temperance Stewart, who ran the house. If there was any work that called for a boy's help, she'd be the one to dole it out.

"Hellooooo! Mrs. Stewart! Helloooooo!" I called. The dogs kept barking. The fact that I could hear but not see them was a bad sign. It meant that they were probably locked inside their kennel, which the Da Souzas almost never did unless no one was home. I listened to their ever more frenzied yelping. I didn't want to waste time, but Mrs. Temperance was my best bet in terms of decent paying work in Sevilla Heights. To settle my indecision I mentally recited a conversion chart I'd learned while studying for the common entrance exams, telling myself that if I got to the end I would leave. *One kilometre equals a thousand metres. One metre equals a hundred centimetres. One mile equals seventeen hundred and sixty yards.* "Helllloooooo! Mrs. Stewart, it's me Bottles!" *One yard equals three feet. One foot equals twelve inches. One litre equals a thousand millimetres.* I gave up once I'd completed the volume and capacity section of the diagram, even though there was still much more to go.

Three yards down, a teenaged princess with a gold anklet, slender ankles, and long, long legs scornfully informed me that her mother wasn't home. I stared a second or two past what was necessary and earned myself a kissed tooth sound of disgust that came nowhere close to denting my lustful armour. "Have a good afternoon," I said with belated respectfulness on my way back out to the street. The image of her, framed in the doorway, lightened my steps past many yards and through two more rejections.

Finally, the man with the dead son and the wife who had moved to Canada offered me ten dollars to weed his garden and take the cutlass to an area of his backyard. I managed to talk him up to thirteen (he steadfastly refused the two dollar jump to fifteen), and set to work. An hour and fifteen minutes later I had my first cash in hand to go with the bag of bottles I'd collected earlier. On my way off of the man with the dead son's property I asked him the time. It was twenty-five after eleven. Half a day to go.

It was mostly a downhill walk into "town" or what my school books would refer to as "St. Paul proper." Along the way I imagined what it would be like if the princess with the golden anklet I'd seen earlier was my girlfriend. Needless to say we'd have sex every day, probably in the evening after she came home from school and hanging out at the new mall with her girl-friends. We'd do other things of course. She wouldn't be as avid a reader as I was, but she'd be perfectly content to massage my scalp and listen to me translate stories as I read to her with my head in her lap. Then I pictured her coming to me distressed after some older boy at her school had refused to take no for an answer and gotten rough with her. The revenge I would take on him became a fantasy in and of itself and by the time I wearily trod into the heart of the city on High Street I was knee-deep in ethereal blood and cradling a Rambo-like machine gun.

"Oh-ho! You think you going stand up in front a me store whole day and beg people bottles? You better fucking move!"

The voice slammed me concrete-hard into reality. I hadn't even realized I was standing in front of Cowboy's Restaurant, a shoddy establishment that added up to little more than a takeout-window and a big, gas oven. Cowboy's ignorance was legendary, as were his fish cakes. I walked off quickly, ignoring four glistening, glass containers I'd spotted a little too late.

After that, falling into the rhythm of my hustle was easy. It all came down to being in motion and being alert. The fast food places were treasure troves. Two garbage bins in somewhat secluded areas were prime targets as long as nobody but the burnouts were around to see. Police headquarters, the bank, and the mall I avoided altogether. Even though the mall parking lot was home to enough bottles to make me rich, the wiry, little man who did security there would give me no chance to collect them. I rode the familiar beats of my routine until it was almost 5 pm and time to make a quick dash over to the recycling plant. Not counting the three I'd broken when I stumbled and fell, I had eighteen bottles I was sure they'd take and two possibles. Four out of my thirteen dollars had gone to buy me a hot corned beef sandwich with egg and cheese, but if I was lucky I could still hit twenty dollars EC before the day was done. If I didn't have to take a bus home, it would be a good day.

Graduation

Fatty, Spiderman, and Plenty-Legs hung upside down from the ceiling in the corner, watching me with all their tiny, insect eyes as I finished buffing my shoes with the big, coarse brush. Behind them, a slight breeze blew in through a chink between the galvanized, zinc wall and the metal roof, causing the silvery web that one or all of the spiders had made to shiver gently in much the way our own home trembled in a strong enough wind. I would have said something to the trio of arachnids, told them where I was going at least, but from her bed at the other end of the two room shanty, Granny P studied me with watery, but focused eyes. She hated me talking to the bugs almost as much as she hated to hear children swear.

"Done now, Granny," I announced, rising to my feet.

"Mmmm, good. Make sure you take up the suit," she rumbled. Her voice had always been deep and it was even deeper now that she was sick. "Sorry boy, you know me min really wan' reach um," she continued on, breathing heavily as she expressed her remorse at not being able to attend my graduation. "Go check Mr. Lee, he guh drive you. Just make sure he nain start drink yet."

Mr. Lee was Granny's "friend" and not a bad man when he was sober. Even with some rum in him he wasn't bad per se, just a little too given to drunken storytelling and non-sexual touchy-feely-ness. In any case, I would rather have ridden with two angry policemen than Granny's friend Mr. Lee.

"Don't worry, Granny," I said.

"Hmph," she replied.

At that point we both knew that I'd be walking the five miles or so to Warwick Primary School. I picked up my suit, which was draped from a wire hanger and covered with a dark green garbage bag. Next I rescued my freshly polished, church/school shoes, holding them in my hand while I slipped into my fastest pair of sneakers (the red ones that were only six months old and had no holes in them).

"G'afternoon, Granny," I smiled, excited now that I was about to finally be on my way.

"Proud ah you," she said, but couldn't manage to return my grin.

I was still floating on the currents of that "proud ah you," drifting on the strength of the earlier "sorry boy" as I made my way over the three square stones that took me from the house to the tiny dirt yard without me having to step in the long, shallow flood ditch that ran along both sides of the street. That Granny P loved me was a given, but for her to apologize to me *and* be proud of me on the same day...that was as rare as the "blue moons" we'd learned about in Language Arts.

On that day, my nameless street was littered with treasure in translucent shades of dark green, clear, and brown, but I resisted the inclination to scoop up the glass nuggets of recyclable gold the way I usually would. This was not a day for the scavenging that had earned me the nickname Bottles. People who graduated at the head of their class didn't go around searching for discarded jars and jugs to haul in for change. Forget about bottle-hunter, I was a valedictorian.

Three blocks later, just before my unnamed street met Cedar Road, I saw that my path was about to be blocked by a quartet of two-footed dragons. No lie, I was immediately nervous. Maybe Damon, or some of the other, tougher boys in my class looked up to the four-pack of bad men that stood between me and my destination, but I despised them. Their de facto leader was a tall, skinny, fair-skinned man (almost to the point of whiteness) known as Fire Reds. Behind him was the regular brawler and sometimes thief known as Cracks, who was as short, muscular, and dark-skinned as Fire Reds was long, stringy, and pale. If it came time to hand out a beating (stabbing, or shooting) it would be Cracks who moved first and Fire Reds who would be the most dangerous. The other two weren't much more than lackeys; even I knew that.

"Eh boy," Fire Reds said when I was within arm's reach, stretching out the word boy so that it carried extra menace and seemed to last forever. I stopped and looked up.

"Tax!" Cracks demanded, stretching out a massive hand with thick, calloused fingers. It was easy to see that palm wrapping around my face, cutting off my air supply and crushing my bones.

"I don't have any money," I protested, trying to sound firm.

"I don't have any money," Reds mimicked in a girlish falsetto. The other laughed, except Cracks. Cracks looked like he was just about ready to slap me.

Senses heightened and time slowed by fear, I smelled the alcohol wafting over from the stocky crook, took a mental photograph of his lanky companion's sneer, heard a single dog (quickly joined by a chorus of others) begin barking in the distance, and heard the beginning strains of Bunji Garlin's "Fiery" playing from a car stereo, all in the time it took me to take a nervous swallow and glance around for any hope of salvation.

I wasn't really expecting help to come; it almost never did, but then…

"Youth man! Oy! Youth!" Somebody was calling, to whom I couldn't immediately tell, but a welcome space had opened up between the four land-dragons and me. Fire Reds was actually sauntering away, slowly though, as if he'd simply lost interest in humiliating an overmatched child. Cracks looked like he still wanted to hit me, but there was an alien uncertainty about him. For the first time ever, I was seeing him hesitate. My heartbeat beginning to slow, I cautiously looked around.

"Youth man!" Came the masculine voice again, this time obviously speaking to me. I stared, unsure whether this was a true reprieve or things were about to get worse. The man approaching didn't look mean. He was dressed in fitted jeans, a designer shirt, and some type of expensive Nikes. Everything about him (from the long, confident stride to the scar under his eye to the slight American twang in his Wadumein patois) said "ghetto-boy-turned-successful-man." He strode easily through the loosening knot of human aggression like a wet comb through kinky hair, pausing only a fraction of a moment to give the still stationary Cracks a stern, questioning glance. The somewhat confused thief took an almost involuntary step backwards and then turned to wander off in search of his crew. My savior shook his head and muttered about "big, grown, useless men." I gave him a shaky, thankful smile.

"Oh yeah," the unknown man said finally, face breaking into a disarming grin. "Now me see you smile, me know you haffu be Lester son. Is true?"

My father's name was Lester Benjamin. When I was six, he and my mother (Tammy Romeo) were hit by a concrete truck and killed instantly on their way home from a Queen of Carnival pageant. I nodded my head in response.

"Knew it!" The man exclaimed, obviously pleased with himself. He immediately offered to drive me home and began to prattle on about how he hadn't seen my father since ninety-two, and was my mother still "little and fine," and he was sure my granny was still as fiery and ornery as ever.

"I guess nobody ever tell you. Them gone man, them pass. Mommy and Daddy both, the two ah them gone. Them been dead a while too," I said, interrupting, then completely stopping the flow of verbiage from his lips.

It was almost as if I'd hit him. The man stood there, leaning unsteadily backwards then forward for several seconds. Perhaps if the situation were different, if I had been informing of someone else's unfortunate death, perhaps then I might have felt some compassion. I was angry instead.

He couldn't of cared that much, I thought as I quickly stomped away, ignoring the belated calls of "sorry man" and "hold on." Nobody ever tell he 'bout what happen to his supposedly close friend? It's not like Wadumein is so big that people wouldn't know to tell him. This ain't New York.

Heated thoughts carried me for a long while. My legs pumped. I ignored the sweat beginning to stain my walking clothes, already resigned to having to freshen up in the boy's washroom once I got to school. Without the usual excitement I felt for its fancy shops, I made my way onto the main strip. I passed the cellphone store advertising "Free Incoming Calls" and the Kentucky Fried Chicken franchise that marked the ghetto's western boundaries. I slipped through laneways stained with political graffiti from anti-government to anti-capitalist and anti-tourism (which to me was just totally crazy, after all we'd learned in school that tourism was the island's only industry). I tiptoed nervously past Rasta men wearing white robes, turbans, and severe expressions. I eavesdropped as I walked behind a group of teenaged girls talking excitedly about their chances of attending a big fete on the nearby island of Grenada. By the time I stopped for a brief rest in the rectangular shade provided by Wong's Lucky Fortune Restaurant, I was beginning to shake the effects of both the petty bullying and the unexpected reminder of my parents.

The combination of a faint breeze and the cool darkness of the building's wide shadow were like heaven. Wishing I had somewhere to rest my good clothes, I leaned against the wall, closed my eyes, and listened to the comforting drone of Wong's radio through the window.

"...as the Milwaukee Bucks drafted point guard

Dwayne Simmons from Syracuse University. As most of you are aware Mr. Simmons was born right here on Wadumein in the parish of St. Thomas and attended Hopetown Primary School before relocating with his parents to the state of New York. Of course, we'd like to send a heartfelt congratulations to the Simmons and Blackman families and especially to you, young Dwayne. Although your time here was brief, Hopetown Primary is an excellent school and I am sure that the things you've learned here at home in Wadumein will serve you well under the bright NBA spotlight."

The announcer went on for a bit longer. Silently, I wished Dwayne Simmons the best. I saw him play once; he was on the island for carnival and a local promoter had set up an exhibition game featuring him and some of his college buddies against an all-local team. He scored fourteen points, dished out nine assists, pulled down five rebounds, and signed my knock-off Cleveland jersey after his team embarrassed the locals. Since then I'd prayed every day that he would fulfill his dream of playing in the NBA. I would fit the young baller in right after I asked God to say "hi" to my parents for me, ease my granny's sickness, and help me keep up my grades. Hearing that he'd gotten drafted felt like a personal victory (even if it was only to the Bucks and not a good team like Cleveland). "Thank you, God," I whispered. I glanced around to ensure that no one was paying me much attention. No one was. Get me off of Wadumein next, I silently added.

The radio had switched to a clip of the Education Minister giving praise to all of the primary and high school students about to graduate, especially those who had done so with honours. My chest swelled with pride, knowing he was talking about and to me.

"...to pay special consideration to those pupils who, by their own merit and diligence, have excelled far beyond the required level of academic and social competence. It comes as no surprise that a significant portion of the island's brightest are or were participants of our Scholastic Achievers' Program. Now, as you most know, the purpose of the S.A.P. is to send students of promise abroad to network, learn, and expand their horizons in the hopes that they will return home and teach what they've learned to their peers. Well, that is exactly what has taken place and I'm pleased to say that many of our S.A.P. participants are already fielding offers from prestigious learning institutions around the world. We send them forward with God's blessing and our best wishes."

I got my back up off the wall and started moving again, my heart light. I was already slated for the Achievers' Program once I started secondary school thanks to the recommendations of a few of my teachers. All I had to do was get good grades the way I'd always done and soon enough it would be me flying out to England, Canada, Brazil, or maybe the States. At that moment, only time and the $3,500 EC I would need to start school stood between me and the world, and if I worked through the summer....

The real money was in lawn care. Recycling bottles would get me anywhere between ten cents and a quarter per container. If Lloydie's Car Wash was short on staff, Lloyd's son Sheldon might give me fifteen dollars for a day's work, but only if there wasn't someone bigger and faster around (and there almost always was). Some of the maids responsible for the busier households were not averse to passing along a dollar or two to help with various chores, mostly running "this thing over so to" Miss. Smith or whoever, but their tasks were often time consuming and seldom paid well. Yeah, the real money was in lawn care, but an army of grown, unemployed men guarded that gate the same way they did so many others. Still, there were those who preferred someone smaller and less intimidating. I put my hopes for the future on finding enough of them to carry me to my goal.

The sun had begun to dip considerably by the time I stepped off of the paved stretch of Old Stone Road and onto the wide, dusty street that led to Warwick Primary School. Several students and their families walked ahead, talking and laughing and taking pictures and remembering when Uncle So and So graduated from this same school or complimenting

Auntie Blah Blah Blah on what a great job she'd done on little What's Her Name's dress. A few, like me, trod alone or in defensive pairs. I consoled myself with the fact that under any other circumstances I'd have Granny here with me, and, in any case, I was the top of my class. A person strong enough to graduate top of the class was surely strong enough to walk in alone.

Jelani Nias (J-Wyze) is the quintessential hype man and emcee. Once a key member of the Soul Controllers, he has a radio background that includes ten years as the dynamic voice of the *Trauma Unit* (Flow 93.5 FM) as well as stints in community & internet radio. J-Wyze also has an unrelenting dedication to the community, which has earned him the Art Starts Upcoming Community Artist Award, the Factor Demo Grant, and the Toronto Arts Council Writers Grant. Born to a jazz musician father who has toured North America and Europe with greats like Toots and the Maytals, and a mother who still sings in an inspirational gospel choir, J-Wyze wanted to be an entertainer for as long as he could remember. After immigrating to Canada from Antigua via Bermuda in 1989 at the age of twelve, J-Wyze began performing at spoken word events in the mid-'90s. He was winner of a Sears Drama Festival acting awards/scholarship, SLAM Poetry competition, and is a published poet and writer.

ALTHEA PRINCE

Push

"And the muscles of his brawny arms
Are strong as iron bands."

The words popped into her head as she enjoyed being wrapped in the arms of this beautiful man. They were a part of the description of the blacksmith in "The Village Blacksmith" by Henry Wadsworth Longfellow. Trivial as the thought was, it came to her now that it had been five years before she understood the meaning of the word "smithy" that was used in the poem. She was a little girl in Antigua when the poem was introduced in school, and no one explained that "smithy" was the same as "blacksmith." They didn't even have blacksmiths in Antigua, and so "smithy" was not a commonplace word in her life.

She eventually found out what the word meant by asking her teacher from England when she got to Fifth Form. She wondered if there were many other children who had read the poem for an assignment and were still none the wiser about the meaning of "smithy." When the teacher had explained that it was simply a derivative of blacksmith, she had felt quite foolish, wondering why such a simple, obvious explanation had not occurred to her. More years later, she realized that the original word did not belong in her world, and she'd been forcefed images of the character and other alien cultural information. She had learned to find enjoyment in such constructs early in her life.

This beautiful man whose arms held her, and whom she held in *her* arms was no *smithy*. He was a schoolteacher, he said…a high school teacher. And he loved to teach. He worked at perfecting the way he communicated with his students he said. He planned the daily lesson way in advance, he told her; and it paid off. Each communication was calculated to have a particular impact and it did. Each thrust was well-timed, finely tuned, and beautifully delivered. That's exactly the way he was making love to her…with thrusts that were well-timed, finely tuned, and beautifully delivered.

The car radio was set at the commercial station, rather than the government-owned station. "It plays more popular music," he said. The car doors were open, so that they could listen to the music as they stood looking at the scenery.

"Antigua is really a very small and very beautiful island," he said. She nodded in agreement, as she looked at the sea crashing against the rocks below. The water was blue-green and translucent. Even from their position at the top of the hill, she could see the clearness of the water and smell the saltiness of it. A fine spray went up in the air each time the water hit the rocks. She thought that this meeting of the water and the land presented a very strong sexual imagery.

"It's as if the sea and the land are mating," she said shyly. She didn't want him to think that she was being purposefully suggestive.

"You sound embarrassed by such a metaphor," he said.

"I am," she admitted. She was clearly embarrassed now, and he laughed at her, hugging her close to his body. She shivered as their bodies made contact.

"Are you cold?" She knew that he fully understood that her shiver was not from the temperature; she could see his understanding in his eyes. He knew that she wanted him. He held her closer, not caring that she could feel his lower body pressed against her. She pressed back, holding him tightly as he kissed her more deeply.

The song on the radio seemed to become louder as they made love. He held her legs up around his waist and penetrated her deeply as the song blared, "Push…push it, push it for me!" He pushed into her even deeper, as if in response to the song's command. She pushed back.

"Push!" The song seemed to go on forever, and so did their lovemaking. She held his head in her hands, revelling in the thick curls of his hair. He had thick-thick hair and it was just a little longer than the style of the time. She was glad of that; she enjoyed the feel of his hair; it was damp now under her hands. He sucked a spot on her neck, just below her earlobe. She whimpered softly at first, and then heard herself making loud cries as their passion mounted.

The sea crashed against the rocks over and over again, and the obvious metaphor now struck her as amusing. Each time the waves dashed themselves against the rocks, she had to work hard not to laugh. The song on the radio seemed louder now, the calypsonian's voice more urgent. "Push it, push it for me!"

"Push!" The radio disc jockey had mixed the music so that the calypso began again at the chorus, "Push! Push it, push it for me!" She turned her head as he leaned down to kiss her and bit him on the neck. He cried out in pain mixed with pleasure. He claimed her lips to prevent her from biting him again. They clung together in ecstasy, moaning into each other's mouths and down their throats, pushing the pulsing energy that they'd created back into their bodies.

The song played on, "Push! Push it, push it for me. Push!" Now they no longer pushed into each other but leaned against each other, exhausted. He nuzzled at her neck again, his lips moist and swollen. He moaned gently as he tried to regain his breath. She lay against him, her face grazing the damp hairs on his chest. She took one of his nipples into her mouth and sucked it gently as if she were nursing on it.

When he whispered, "I love you," she didn't know what to say. She wanted to reply, "I love you too," but the words stuck in her throat. She did feel that she was in love with him but she argued with herself. How could it be love? They'd only met each other the night before. In all the years that they had seen each other, that was the first time they had ever even had a conversation. She filled her mouth more completely with his nipple and moaned softly. She hoped that he would accept that as an adequate response.

Six months later, she received her letter of acceptance to go to Saint Leo University in Florida. When she told him that she would be going away to college, his face fell.

"What? When did you decide to go?" The questions followed each other closely. He seemed annoyed.

"Last year," she answered.

"Why you didn't tell me before this? You knew for so long and you never said anything about this to me? Why?"

She felt guilty and trapped. Why hadn't she told him earlier? She knew that she had chosen not to tell him but had no clear explanation for her choice. He drummed his fingers on the steering wheel of the car. A muscle in his neck jumped. He gritted his teeth as if to control that muscle, but still it jumped. She touched his arm; he did not respond. She kissed his cheek where the line of his jaw was taut. She kissed his earlobe and then pushed the tip of her tongue into his ear. He shivered despite himself, responding involuntarily to her caress. She saw her advantage and took it. She stabbed her tongue in and out of his ear, noting with appreciation that he always had such clean ears. She reached into his shirt and tweaked his nipple. He stretched his legs out and moaned softly, but she could feel him holding himself in check.

"I love you," she surprised herself by saying it. She had still never once told him "I love you" unless he said it first. "I'll never leave you; I'll never be with anyone else, even though I'll be away."

"But you'll be in Florida for at least three years!" His voice sounded strained and plaintive, as if tears lurked nearby. She looked up at him. He *was* crying, the tears running down his cheeks.

"Sweetheart, don't cry," she said, trying to comfort him, "I'll come home during holidays." She held him in her arms again, thinking, "He feels like my baby." She put her thoughts into words, "Baby, I love you. You're my baby." He snuggled into her arms at her words, and she held him closer enjoying the motherly feelings that his emotions had generated in her. She felt strong and powerful. It occurred to her that her feelings were a little sick, but at the same time, she liked having them.

She had not had this sense of power in their relationship before. Always, he had been in charge and always she had let him be in charge, revelling in the fact that he was a strong Antiguan man. Now, her strong Antiguan man was showing her his soft side. She didn't think of tears as weakness, but as gentleness; yet still, they gave her a sense of power.

Her thoughts made her uncomfortable at the same time that they gave her pleasure. She tried to shut them out, and lowering her head, kissed his thick hair; at the same time, her hands moved to caress his face. He snuggled even deeper into her arms and turned sideways so that he could fit his upper body into her lap. She opened her legs and enfolded him with her whole body. The energy changed from sadness to the passion that always ignited so easily between them. It was as if their hearts remembered being together in some eternal emotional connection. She always told herself that there had to be some kind of past-life connection to make their closeness so strong.

"Don't leave me," he said as he received her kisses on his eyelids, on his nose, on his lips. "Don't leave me sweetness; stay until next year, then I can go to Florida with you."

"Really?" She was surprised. He had never mentioned wanting to go to live in Florida. Suddenly, she didn't feel so strong and powerful any more.

"Yes," he sounded a little embarrassed. "I applied

to Florida State to do a diploma in Marine Biology. I want to be able to help our fisheries industry. I've applied to go next year."

For a while she did not speak. Then after a time, she found her voice, "And when were *you* going to tell *me*?" It was a rhetorical question, but she demanded an answer. "Just when were you going to tell me about *your* plans?"

She lost the sense of power that she had felt a few moments earlier. All this time, he was planning to leave Antigua and he never told her. Imagine that!

"I suppose we're the same," he said, "both of us didn't tell everything." Her last feelings of strength and power ebbed away in a tide of disappointment. "Yes, we are alike," she said, "exactly alike."

She felt her tears cold and wet on the hot skin of her face. He held her comfortingly in his arms with a fatherly embrace. He felt strong and powerful as he took his big, open hand and wiped away her tears. She realized that things were back to normal. She wondered how long they would last.

They Buried Her Mother Twice

She can still remember how it felt the first time she saw the shoe-trees in Townline, just outside of Orangeville. She captured the whole experience in her senses, and in her mind and heart. As they approached Orangeville, her friend who was driving, told her about a shoe-tree that was near to the town. "In fact, it's really just west of Orangeville…in Townline, pretty near to where I grew up," he said. "This is no ordinary tree. Several years ago—in 1972, to be exact—someone began to tie shoes onto the tree, for no reason known to anyone." Her friend spoke quite matter-of-factly, as if it was normal.

"In fact," her friend said, enjoying the intense interest she was showing in hearing about the shoe-tree, "there are now several shoe-trees."

She wanted to tie a pair of shoes to the trees, but she hadn't had sufficient notice. Before she knew it, the tree was upon them, and she wasn't about to relinquish her precious, expensive running shoes. There were six trees altogether—all bearing the same strange fruit. The tree made her think of Billie Holiday's song

"Strange Fruit" that referred to the gruesome lynching of Black men, hanging from trees, the victims of white racism in the southern United States.

After the Orangeville trip, she became quite obsessed with the idea of tying a pair of shoes on one of the shoe-trees, but she faced a dilemma: if she were to tie a pair of shoes on the tree, she felt that they ought to have some meaning for her. She could not, however, bear the thought of not being able to look at any of the shoes that were significant to her. That would soon change; and the right shoes came along rather unexpectedly.

It started out as an ordinary funeral. Some people sang hymns in between weeping quietly in their handkerchiefs. There were some who stood, dry-eyed, stoically singing the hymns that the family had selected. "Nearer, My God, To Thee" and "Sunset and Evening Star." That last hymn was torturous, as no one really knew the tune well enough to carry it without the piano or organ. Nonetheless, the whole family carried on singing it, triumphantly harmonizing the last verse together—determined to do this last thing for their mother, grandmother, and aunt. They knew that she had always said that it was a beautiful hymn.

Her mother had said a lot of things to her…some were good, and most were hurtful. She once told her that she was too clumsy to wear high heels; and believing her, she never did. For her mother's funeral, however, she decided that she would wear high heels— just to spite her. She didn't own a pair of high heels, so the day before she got on the plane to go from Toronto to Antigua for the funeral, she went out and bought a pair of white patent-leather-high-heeled shoes. She teetered around the store in them, and told herself that she'd be fine.

Well, there they were, awaiting the minister's return from visiting the prisoners. He'd said he'd be a little late…but it was a good hour later, and they were tired of the singing and the crying, and the pauses, and the singing again….They sang the Lord's Prayer for a third time. They were becoming quite good at it, Mertle thought. Maybe if the minister didn't arrive for another hour, they would be as good as a choir at singing the Lord's Prayer.

"Our Father, who art in hea-a-a-a-ven, Hallow-ed be-e-e Thy name. Thy ki-i-ing-dom come, Thy will be done, on Earrrr-th, as it is in Hea-a-a-a-ven. Give us this da-a-y our daily bread…." Everyone sang that last line with real feeling. She suspected that they were hungry. Her mind wandered to the simple fare they'd ordered from the caterers…they would never be able to feed everyone with that. They had planned to serve an afternoon snack, but if the minister didn't arrive soon, they'd be running into the dinner hour. She thought of the possibility of a miracle happening. Like Jesus' four loaves and five fishes; or was it five loves and four fishes? Maybe the food would stretch somehow; and while they couldn't pull a loaves-and-fishes-thing, they just might leave everyone satisfied. Her final wish for a miracle was that her feet would stop hurting in the white patent-leather-high-heeled shoes.

Someone struck up "Amazing Grace" maybe for the third time, and the group wearily went along, dragging out the last notes of each line into a purposefully mournful wail. There was no mistaking it: people were hungry and tired. Mertle was all of those things, and she was also in pain. Her feet hurt in the high-heeled shoes, because they were new, and because high heels are ridiculous things for anyone to wear. And they hurt her in particular because her bones just weren't made to be teetering on high heels. She was an angular woman, with big hips, a wide pelvis, and sturdy pelvic bones. She needed good support on the ground.

She could feel her pelvis being drawn up to some other place; and the muscles in her calves ached. Her arches, her instep, and her knees were all crying out for salvation. She was a right mess in the foot department. She looked down at the white patent-leather-high-heeled shoes, and they seemed to be winking up at her with laughter—her mother's laughter. "You're too clumsy to wear high heels." Well, she thought, on this day, at this funeral, Mother Dear, you're quite right! And suddenly, she didn't care at all about wearing high-heeled shoes. She wished that she could rewind the clock to the day before she'd bought them; and she wished that she had worn her nice, flat loafers. And then another thought struck her slam-bam in the middle of her forehead: she didn't care about winning with her mother any more. The war was over!

The gathering sang on. Her mother's cousin, who, because of his love of sailing was nicknamed "Uncle Boatswain," started up a rousing chorus of "Red Sails In the Sunset, Way Out On the Sea." You could hear the liquor from the "Wake" from the night before, and you could see the aftermath on him as well. They got through to the second line: "Oh, carry my loved one home safely to me" before someone pointed out that it was not a hymn. Uncle Boatswain was undaunted. He droned on by himself, raising his voice to fill up the whole graveyard of the church: "She sailed at the dawning, all day I've been blue-ooo! Red sails in the sunset, I'm trusting in you." Satisfied that he had done his bit for his cousin, Uncle Boatswain stopped singing, and looked around with a pleased look on his face. Some of his relatives smiled at him understandingly, others glared at him for desecrating the sacredness of the gravesite with his everyday song. Uncle Boatswain rose to the occasion, and started up the Lord's Prayer again. Everyone droned on behind him; this time, there was an undeniable passion in the way they harmonized the words: "…Give us this day our daily bread."

An impetuous act by an older, relative with an alpha male kind of personality soon shifted everything. It only took a few moments, but as Mertle watched it happening, she felt as if it took a lot longer. Things seemed to be moving in slow motion. She watched the man go into what she knew he proudly would call his "take-charge" role. She wasn't quite sure how he was related to her mother, but she had a vague memory of her mother introducing him to them as Cousin somebody's son. He posed what she thought was a rhetorical question: Why not have the burial done by Pastor Black who had come from St. Kitts for the funeral of his old friend? Mind you, Pastor Black's church was not an Anglican church, but that minor detail did not matter. In a flash, her mother was buried by Pastor Black.

The hymns were sung, the first layer of sod thrown, and final hymns were in full swing when the real minister of the church came charging into the churchyard. He was in grand performance style, singing with the group as he approached the gathering. His fresh, white robes flowed behind him in the breeze, and there was a vibrancy about him. He was looking forward to performing at this funeral. Then he saw that "his body" had already been buried, and he went ape shit! How dare they carry out an interment of the body in his absence? "I told you people that I would be late, as I was visiting the prison today."

So—they buried her mother twice. They didn't dig her up, but the real minister did the prayers that he was supposed to do while they all stood tensely with their heads bowed as if in prayer. In reality, some of them were really angry; others were very amused, and were stifling laughter. Mertle wanted to laugh but she didn't think that would have gone down very well with the minister…or with anyone, for that matter. Later, others told her that they stifled laughter at the unbelievable situation of someone being buried by two ministers of the church—two different churches!

To Mertle's surprise, she felt need of her mother to comfort her at that moment; perhaps more than she had ever wanted her. She had never had comfort from her in life anyway, but it sure was a moment when she heard her heart yearning for her mother to tell her that everything was all right. It would have been a first!

After the second set of prayers from the second minister, the whole gathering began to make their way to their cars. As she turned to walk away, teetering in her white patent-leather-high-heeled shoes, Mertle found herself taking care not to step on any freshly turned soil. She didn't want to arrive at the reception in soiled shoes, but she also had another reason for avoiding the graveyard soil. Her mother always told her to clean the dirt of cemeteries off your shoes before going inside your house.

Just then, a chocolate brown stone, the same colour as her mother's skin, winked up at her laughingly from the gravesite. She accepted that everything had been arranged in the realm of spirit, and considered it a final farewell from her mother. She thought of how she had managed to be in control of things, even in death. She picked up the stone, and put it in her handbag, saying under her breath "Goodbye, Mother; it's over. You're not in charge anymore."

In her car on the way back to town, no one spoke as she manoeuvred the twists and turns of the narrow country roads taking her carload of relatives to the reception hall. Yet, she could feel a collective sigh of relief rippling around her.

When she got back to Toronto, she put the chocolate brown stone on the mantelshelf—all by itself. She wondered how her mother felt being all alone. She knew what being all alone felt like. Had she not felt all alone as a child, even though she had three brothers and two sisters? She believed that her mother too had felt all alone, even though she had six children, a husband, and a large supply of grandchildren.

As she unpacked her suitcase, she looked at the white patent-leather-high-heeled shoes that she had allowed old anger to prompt her into purchasing. She knew exactly where they were going to reside in as short a time as it would take for her to drive there. She also knew that she would bury her mother yet a third time when she hung those shoes on one of the shoe trees in Townline, near to Orangeville.

Although it was dark, she easily found a space on one of the shoe trees for her white patent-leather-high-heeled shoes. A pair of fancy, white, dance shoes peeped out at her from the darkness. They were on the original tree, and she noticed only now that they were just like a pair that her older cousin who had returned to live in Antigua used to wear to dance halls in the old days. She had lived in England, and she would boast about how she was a frequent favourite in the dance halls in London. She never quite adjusted to life in Toronto. Eventually, she had returned to Antigua, and settled in there quite happily.

The white dance shoes seemed to wink at her now from their perch on the tree branch, and she decided that they would be appropriate companions for her white patent-leather-high-heeled shoes. After she nailed her shoes to the tree branch, she stood for a moment, admiring her handiwork. She chuckled softly, and whispered, "Goodbye, Mother." Then she drove back to Toronto. She had closed a chapter.

Award-winning author Dr. Althea Prince has taught sociology at York University and the University of Toronto. She now teaches at Ryerson University, in the G. Raymond Chang School of Continuing Education. During the years 2002 to 2005, Prince was Managing Editor of the publishing company Canadian Scholars' Press & Women's Press. She has just completed an academic year as Writer-in-Residence for the Toronto District School Board's Just Read It Programme and is Writer-in-Residence at Newcomer Women's Services (NEW) Toronto.

Dr. Prince's publications include:

The Politics of Black Women's Hair
Ladies of the Night: Stories

Feminisms & Womanisms.

　A Women's Studies Reader (Co-edited)

Loving This Man (novel)

Being Black (essays)

Awards:

Ryerson University Faculty Award – The Kay Livingstone Award. 2011.

Outstanding Person of the Year – The Antigua Girls' High School Alumni Association of North America. New York, U.S.A. 2010.

The First Annual Award for Literary Excellence – The Antigua and Barbuda International Literary Festival. 2007.

Prime Minister of Antigua and Barbuda's Jubilee Award for Outstanding Contributions and Achievements in the Field of Arts and Culture. 2006.

The Canadian Children's Book Centre "CHOICE AWARD" for children's book: *How the East-Pond Got Its Flowers.* 1991.

DJANET SEARS

Thomasina, Angel, and Me

I. Thomasina

There's a respectable negro woman, lives in my house. She's got work to do, things to get done. She rarely notices the moon and never sees the sun. Thomasina hides her 'fro under a Diahann Carroll Kanekalon wig she ordered from *Jet* magazine. She stares at P's and Q's most all day long. Make no mistake though, she's twenty-first century negro. She don't "Yes, ma'am. No, ma'am," no one, no how. She's got her own three bags, and they're full of dreams. 'Stead of fussing and cussing, she just bites her lip and keeps her mouth closed. Though when she ain't wearing lipstick you'd swear there was a hole right there. Fools say all manner of shit to Thomasina and she won't say a word. She knows. She knows that if she don't tie her tongue someone's bound get hurt, and that someone is usually her.

Angel is Thomasina's daughter. She lives in my house too. Someone needs to tell that woman the sixties done come and gone. She is all hair. You'd think she was auditioning for the lead in a Cleopatra

Jones action flick. She's all mouth too. Don't tell her nothing, 'cause she ain't even 'fraid of dying. She didn't get the memo 'bout this being a post-racial era. She's always on about privilege this and oppression that. Thomasina don't talk to Angel. Hasn't said a word to her going on twenty years.

Some fool at work had been flinging microaggressions at Thomasina. Finally he accused her of plagiarizing a poem she had printed in the staff newsletter. No proof. No nothing. Kept telling everyone on the floor, in his erudite opinion, she was claiming other people's work as her own.

Thomasina comes home, muttering up all under her breath. Angel, 'bout fifteen then, hugs her mama like fifteen year olds can when they have a mind to. Her mama starts to talk, spillin' beans, sauce—Hell, the enchilada's on the floor. Didn't Angel skip school next day, threaten the fool with a knife. In public. Cops, court, lawyers, juvenile detention, two years. Dayam. Thomasina tremble cried taking that dream outta her bag.

Thomasina won't complain 'bout the constant invalidations. She's a crusty old thing. She can take it. Least so she say. She has to. Sure sometimes she'll ask the friendly woman who works beside her if she saw the shadow in the water, smelled the sour fish. But her neighbour only smelled the sea breeze and salt air. Told Thomasina she'd confused the smell of ocean with rotting shadows. Thomasina would nod, as if to say, yeah; smile, as if to say, how silly of me.

She keeps her wig on in my house does Thomasina. But I know she takes it off when the sun goes down. I've seen her go for walks, her super coils free as the leaves dancing. She lets the air through her head, her brain. She breathes slow and hopes no-one sees her shake just a little. She's fragile walking at night with her hair free. So she don't do it often. And no one better look at her sideways like you want to call her Cassius Clay, when she already told you her name was Muhammad Ali, or she'll wipe that simile right off your face, and what she's been holding will come retching up if you even hint that anything about her is in no way enough, when it wasn't meant for you.

It was meant for all who'd told her all day long that her things were not her own. Who told her that her perception of the world was wrong, that they hadn't noticed her in the book they'd read on the subject and gave her a number to call to get a better understanding of her own experiences, her feelings. Someone who could help her reinterpret the world appropriately.

If you catch Thomasina with the breeze at her back and her hair dancing free... Let her be.

II. Angel

Angel loves Thomasina. She sets a bath for her most evenings. It's Angel who helps her remove the armour, unpins the wig, sets the dark and sassy crown on the faceless white Styrofoam head, unbraids her mama's hair and with her fingers coaxes the blood into her scalp, her mind. And still Thomasina don't say nothing at all. Though Angel don't stop talking none. She's speechifying all day long. If it ain't her job, it's the teacher at night school, the bus driver, the security guard that followed her through the department store, the police, the system, racism, sexism, classism, heterosexism, white supremacy.

They share the same bed, Thomasina and Angel. Don't matter that Thomasina's turned away, her ears stuffed with cotton. Angel's yapping all night long. She hardly ever gets a wink of sleep does Angel. Seems she don't want anyone else to neither.

III. Me

I lie between them wondering what I'm gonna do. We share the same pillow do Thomasina, Angel, and me. We share the same head too.

Christmas Eve

For eleven and a half months, I long,
yearn for it even. Not the shops—I hate
the shops—excursions through a sea
of swarming hordes in search of that perfect
gift, mouth-watering delicacies. Every
year we haul three hundred thousand tons of festive
fare, most of which goes straight to my hips,
and takes three months of concerted effort
to remove. Still, for eleven months I dream:

The gathering, the cooking, the singing.
Sisters, husbands, children, cousins, parents,
all camped out at my sister's place from Christmas
Eve till the first day of the new year, to eat,
drink, shout, cry, laugh, slam down dominoes, cheat
at euchre, argue about the three-minute timer
my sister uses at the Scrabble board.

On Christmas Eve once the cornbread
graces the oven, and sweet smells wind
their way up stairways, under door jambs,
through keyholes, it begins:

Amen.
Amen.
A-men. Amen. Amen.
Mary had a baby.
Amen.
Wrapped in a swaddling.
Amen.
Christmas morning.
A-men. Amen. Amen

A pot and wooden spoon. Dry
rice and bean filled Tupperware
and mason jars provide the groove.
Three dusty guitars magically
emerge. Christian and agnostic sing.

   Silent night. Holy—

Dad plucking out chords on fingers
grown too thick for the strings.

   Sleep in heavenly peace,
   sleep in heavenly—

Golden cornbread removed
from the oven, so fragrant
it permeates our beings.

   I heard the bells on Christmas—

Turkey surfaces from the spicy brine,
to carefully loosen the breast skin,
layer and massage with herbed butter
on which to delicately arrange fresh bay
leaves and sage in a mosaic.

And wild and sweet the words repeat
Of peace on earth—

Score the ham, pierce with garlic, thyme,
marjoram, peppers. My sister serves Jamaican
patties and black pudding. The adults sip
on Baileys or ten-year-old rum. Make the punch:
One sour, two sweet, three strong, four weak.

Drink the rum on a Christmas morning,
Drink a rum.
Moma drink if you drinking.

And...

Jean and Dinah,
Roseta and Clementina.

Not only Christmas songs anymore. Sup
the pepper pot strong with casreep and sugar.

Edelweiss. Edelweiss.
Every morning you greet—

Us in as close to full harmony
as we can muster. Welcome
every note out of key. Jerk
the chicken. Fry the fish.
season the curry goat, soak
the salted-fish for the ackee
and roast breadfruit Christmas morning.

O holy night! The stars are brightly shining,
It is the night of the dear—

The kids rehearse play planned
for the lighting of the Kwanzaa
candles: green, black, and red.

Long lay the world in sin and error pining,
Till He appears—

I place the turkey in a large container
to sit in the great Canadian refrigerator
outdoors, under a crate, so the raccoons
can't get at it. Pray it won't freeze
like two years ago. We spent most
of Christmas day with the turkey submerged
in warm water, which erased all trace

of herbs and marinade. The laughter
at recollecting when the oven caught on fire.

Fall on your knees,
Oh, hear the angel—

We try to remember those not here this year. Honour
those who've passed and won't be with us again. Quietly
taking imaginary pictures so that we might recall in
case, God
forbid, this is the last Christmas of a sister, a husband,
a cousin, a parent. We take imaginary pictures
and try to make this Christmas last forever.

O night divine. O night divine!

Celebrated playwright Djanet Sears is also an acclaimed theatre director and an adjunct professor in drama at the University of Toronto. Her plays have been widely produced, published and even translated. Selected productions include: *The Adventures of a Black Girl in Search of God* (Mirvish Productions, Nightwood Theatre, Obsidian Theatre); *Harlem Duet* (The Stratford Shakespeare Festival, St. Louis Black Repertory Company, Nightwood Theatre, CanStage), and *Afrika Solo* (Black Theatre Workshop, Factory Theatre, Theatre Fountainhead). She is also the editor of two anthologies: *Testifyin': Contemporary African Canadian Drama, Vols. I & II*. She has been a visiting fellow at Stanford University, a Creative Fellow at the Royal Shakespeare

Company and Warwick University, Playwright-in-Residence at Tarragon Theatre, Factory Theatre, Nightwood Theatre, and International Artist-in-Residence at the Joseph Papp Public Theatre in New York City. Her honours include the Governor General's Literary Award, the Canadian Screenwriting Award, the Gold Prize at the International Radio Festival Of New York, a Chalmers Fellowship, a Martin Luther King Jr. Achievement Award, the Toronto Arts Foundation William Kilbourne Award, the African Canadian Achievement Award, the Harry Jerome Award, and the Floyd S. Chalmers Canadian Play Award.

MANSA TROTMAN

Listen

I am one
classified as one of them all
classified in terms of what I'm not
of what supposedly limits me
somehow qualified to speak on the
feelings of politicians, "leaders," criminals, friends,
and ancestors
(because of course they're all the same)
but I'm me
what will you call me?
non-white (what is that?)
visible minority (invisible?)
black, brown, coloured
(don't miss a spot...hope you don't go outside the
lines)
light-skinned, dark-skinned
boxed and packaged, cut and scraped
until I fit into some sort of mould
that calms you and makes you feel more comfortable
don't worry, you're using the right term
this week

until it (or I) no longer fits
outgrew that one
gotta think of something else
until I leave that one behind as well
and you have to catch me cause
I'm flying
over lumps and clumps of your classifications
look closely and you'll find that
they're people
real people
who you lumped and clumped
together from the beginning
only you called them a different name
a different term
some classification
and they're still here
can't classify them into oblivion
can't limit them until they can't think
because we will still be here
defying classifications.

Marrow

There is no more love to be drained from these bones
You have sucked the marrow dry
And nothing is left save for three beads of sweat
On foreheads where kisses were once laid to rest

Sundays

i. miss him. mostly on Sundays
When phones don't ring

he. suffers silently. for the lies
he told and deception he sold

we. were friends. and now
there are just ghosts

i. marvel endlessly. that what I thought
was my life can now be written
as a single poem.

Mansa Trotman is a writer whose work grips her audience and readership in the gut, wrings it, and then moves on to elicit laughter...all in the same heartbeat. She moved from the spoken word forums to video renditions of her early poetry, then later, publishing in several anthologies. Her first poems were published when she was a teenager in high school in an early African Canadian publication: *Ember Magazine*. Mansa Trotman's most recent publication is entitled, *the space*

that connects us. (TSAR Publishers, Toronto, Fall 2012).

Mansa Trotman's poetry is included in the following anthologies:

Mercury Retrograde and other Stories by Women. Authors: Camille Hernandez-Ramdwar, Sharon Lewis, Mansa Trotman, Ruba Nadda. (Sister Vision Press, 1999)

Word Up. Spoken Word Poetry in Print. Edited by Jill Battson and Ken Norris. (Key Porter Books, 1995)

Black Girl Talk. Edited by "The Black Girls." (Sister Vision Press, 1995)